Give Joy to My Youth

TERESA GALLAGHER

Give Joy
to My Youth

A Memoir of Dr. Tom Dooley

NEW YORK
FARRAR, STRAUS AND GIROUX

To the Heirs of Doctor Tom Dooley

This book is dedicated to all the members of The Thomas A. Dooley Foundation at home and in the field, who have given of themselves in mercy and time, and shared their art and skill with their neighbors.

Doctor Dooley's heirs are the compassionate doctors, nurses, airline stewardesses, and plain people everywhere who in his words are "dedicating some of their lives to the service of others."

CONTENTS

ILLUSTRATIONS

Illustrations

ix

Illustrations

Dr. Verne Chaney and Bob Considine with Marlene Thompson at benefit dinner.

Marlene Thompson, on leave from Pan American, at Tibetan refugee school.

The first benefit party of the New York City Chapter.

Peggy Lee with Frank Schait and the Dalai Lama's brother. Miss Lee's dog was a gift from Tibetans.

Peter Purdy at the Tibetan handicraft training center.

Dr. Virginia Singleton and Vernell Geistweidt, R.N. in India.

The Foundation's health unit at work with a native doctor in northern India.

Dr. David Stanley, Khong Island, Laos.

Dr. Theodore Reich and Zola Watson, R.N. at Nepal.

Jean Ennis, R.N., first member of the Dooley Youth League to become a nurse.

Dr. Jose Castallanos at Ban Houei Sai.

Dr. Richard Baldwin, Ban Houei Sai, Laos.

Delores Frank, United Air Lines stewardess, instructs Lao student nurses.

Dr. James Dinneen of Portland, Oregon and family before departure for Laos.

Foreword

Tom Dooley was an ordinary man—an ordinary citizen, an ordinary doctor, and an ordinary believer. The one unusual thing about Tom was that he was a doer. He acted out his manhood, his responsibilities as a citizen, his Hippocratic oath as a doctor, and his faith in God. This great nation of America was created by such ordinary men doing extraordinary things. In these days of fear, unrest and violence in a world where men yearn more for mere survival than for freedom, Tom Dooley left a legacy of hope and example to people in America and throughout the world.

The Thomas A. Dooley Foundation was created four years ago to continue to act out that legacy as a group of ordinary Americans, confident in themselves, proud of their country, and determined to take an active part in the world. They are a group not just concerned with their own security and comfort, but wanting to give of themselves and their skills so that other peoples in the world, responding to their new-found freedom, might come to know a better life. Their goal is a world of friendship and understanding, not one of war and hate. As Dr. Tom Dooley believed, the tools for achieving this goal are education and medicine.

Those people of The Thomas A. Dooley Foundation now working in the villages of Asia, those working in chapters and youth leagues across the U.S. are—like Tom

Dooley—ordinary people. They are doers and—also like Tom—they are splendid Americans. God bless them.

VERNE CHANEY, M.D.
Executive Director
The Thomas A. Dooley Foundation, Inc.

Preface

Though several years have passed since Dr. Tom Dooley died, there are people who still think of him as a living person. I recently received a postcard forwarded by Cardinal Spellman's office; it was written by a young lady who had addressed it to *"Dr. Tom Dooley, St. Patrick's Cathedral, New York."* There is also the case of a young ballet dancer in New Jersey who recently discovered Dr. Dooley's books and sent me a huge box of medical supplies for the hospitals in Asia now supported by The Thomas A. Dooley Foundation; as if to someone living, her card read: "To Tom with love from Deirdre." Though he is no longer a living person, Dr. Dooley is still a living force, as I hope to demonstrate further in this book.

Dr. Dooley's work has always appealed to people of all faiths. One could say he was an early worker in the ecumenical movement. Through his efforts in foreign lands, he was also one of the forerunners of the Peace Corps, and it is known that in 1960 President-elect John F. Kennedy discussed his plans for this great organization with Dr. Dooley. Dr. Dooley's work among the people of southeast Asia not only provided a model for some of the aims of the Peace Corps, but may have been one of its inspirations. It is also known that Dr. Dooley was one of the people under consideration for the position of director of the Peace Corps, despite the fact that his illness was well known and he had already had his first operation.

Dr. Dooley's death early in 1961, at the age of 34 years and one day, was a severe blow to many young people who saw in him a hero and an idealist. An idealist is often classified, derisively, as a "do-gooder," and there often seems to be an uphill fight in store for the man of high ideals who truly wants to achieve. Tom fought this fight successfully, and his sincerity, his humor, and his idealism won the hearts of people all over the world. He was loved by the young, particularly in America. From their letters I have learned how determined young people are that his memory and his work shall not be consigned to the dustbin and, after four years, this is a very comforting realization.

When Tom was alive, his energy, dedication and determination resulted in hectic moments; things would often be in a turmoil, and he constantly worried that all sorts of jobs that *ought* to be done were not being done. His sense of urgency never deserted him. Life should have calmed down for us in The Thomas A. Dooley Foundation by this time, and it seems rather strange that we still find ourselves in a minor crisis every now and then. I would be less than honest if I did not admit that even now I instinctively call on Tom to "do something" to help us in our and his work.

The title of this book, *Give Joy to My Youth,* is taken from the opening antiphon of the Ordinary of the Mass: "I will go to the altar of God, to God who gives joy to my youth." As a young boy and during his college days, Dr.

Dooley served as an acolyte (at Notre Dame he served the six A.M. Mass for years). I remember that when Tom told me this was one of his favorite responses in the Mass, I thought at the time, "That might make a good title for a book."

Joy and joyous are the words that characterized the life and work of Dr. Tom Dooley. His sense of humor was surpassed only by his dedication. Tom's darkest moments were lightened by his faith and trust, and his courage gave joy to fellowmen locked in self-pity, apathy, and defeat. I hope that this book will move all people, and particularly young people, to accept their own burdens and to give a helping hand to the other fellow's burden.

Often Tom reminded me that "the reward for service is the strength to serve." You will find in this book stories of greatness, and of ordinary people doing extraordinary things—people from all walks of life, all faiths, and all ages. In this book I hope to tell you of some of the experiences I shared with Dr. Dooley, and how his work is being continued. I only pray that it proves worthy of a truly great man and a wonderful dear friend.

I wish to acknowledge my indebtedness to many people for their encouragement and support in writing this book. First and foremost, I am most grateful to Mrs. Agnes E. Dooley, Dr. Dooley's mother. When I first told her that I had been asked to write a book, she wrote (January 10, 1964): "I, too, think the work you have done among the teenagers is fabulous, and I would like to see a big success made of your book. As I told you before, you have my blessings . . . You know much about those years we all spent together—some of it very humorous, and some of it very sad. Whatever I can do to help with this book of yours, I will gladly undertake." My only regret is that the book was not ready before Mrs. Dooley's death in the summer of 1964.

I am also grateful to the late F. W. Ecker, former president of the Metropolitan Life Insurance Company, whose generous response to Dr. Dooley's first letter gave the initial impetus to my volunteer work with the doctor; to Malcolm Dooley and the Dr. Dooley Estate for permission to quote the doctor's letters; to James E. McGurk, my former boss, and Joseph J. Carney, my present boss, for their patient understanding; to Charles Christiernin, whose early interest in our efforts made many things possible for us; to Audrey Byrne, whose nimble fingers, close scrutiny of my manuscript, and enthusiasm helped me to follow through; to Paul Hellmuth, for his excellent advice; to Margaret Alberding, R.N., Dr. Richard Baldwin, Richard Blanchefield, Robert Copenhaver, Sr. Mary Corinne, O.P., Mother Doyle, Mrs. Bryan Edwards, Betty Moul, Most Rev. Bishop Fulton J. Sheen, Dr. David Stanley, Miss Mildred Walden, Most Rev. John P. Walsh, O.M.I., and others for permission to quote from their letters; to Sister Mary Lucilla, R.C.D., for her words of encouragement; and to Father E. Paul Amy, S.J., for his guidance at trying moments.

I also wish to thank the Honorable Khamchan Pradith, the Permanent Observer from Laos to the United Nations, and a dear friend of Dr. Dooley's, for translating the letter from Savath's students; Mrs. Eugene Kormendy, for her undying interest in Tom's work and her support of this book; my sister, Mrs. Agnes McDonough, for help I can never adequately repay; my editor at Farrar, Straus and

Giroux for his editorial advice; all the members of the Dr. Dooley Aid Club in our company; our dear friends in Massachusetts, the unrelated Linehans, Gertrude and Annie T.; to John Creedon; to those faithful members of the New York City Chapter and to our past and present members of the Board of Trustees who are not mentioned only because of lack of space; and finally, Dr. Verne Chaney, who in his deep sense of dedication as Executive Director of The Thomas A. Dooley Foundation has borne the main burden of helping to continue Dr. Dooley's work. I wish to add that I intend to contribute from the royalties of this book to The Thomas A. Dooley Foundation, the only organization carrying on Dr. Dooley's concept of person-to-person medical work.

T.G.

Give Joy to My Youth

Chapter I

THE OFFICE WITH THE
RED DOOR

"I am only one, but I am one. I cannot do everything, but I can do something. What I can do, I ought to do, and what I ought to do, by the grace of God, I will do." I sit here typing these wonderful words in a penthouse office on the 20th floor of 220 Fifth Avenue, the address of the New York City Chapter of The Thomas A. Dooley Foundation. What has brought *me* here, and why have others made sacrifices to work here? What set of circumstances prompted one of our girls to carry a scrub pail and brush to clean up this office on a holiday, when she could have been enjoying her leisure elsewhere? What inspires our workers to carry endless shopping bags, and to put on their "Foundation" hats and start their volunteer work?

Now in its fourth year, our Chapter has been growing steadily from the central core provided by the group of volunteers who originally worked closely with Dr. Dooley. What kind of human beings are they, and by what roads have they arrived here? For instance, there is Betty Moul. In 1959, when she first heard of the doctor's illness, she called him at Memorial Hospital and said, "Dr. Dooley, I can type. Perhaps I can help you in some way. Do you need me?" Though Tom thanked her politely, he was noncommittal and Betty decided to call on him at the hospital. When Dr. Dooley looked up and said, "Who are you?", Betty told him she had phoned him earlier and wanted to know if she could help. The word "help" always had magic connotations for Tom, and he said, "You'd better see Teresa Gallagher." Betty is now the secretary of Senator Jacob Javits of New York. From the moment she originally volunteered, she has never been anything but one of the most dedicated workers in The Thomas A. Dooley Foundation.

In 1964 Betty saved enough money to go abroad and see at first hand the programs run by the Foundation, and her greatest dream was realized when she made her way up to northern Laos for a visit to the hospital at Ban Houei Sai. Earlier, on the first leg of this trip, she had stopped at the Foundation's projects at Mussoorie and Dharmsala, India. When she arrived at Mussoorie, where Peter and Susan Purdy were conducting classes and building a handicraft center under the aegis of the Foundation for the benefit of the Tibetan refugees, she emptied her overweight suitcase of all the Dooley kits, socks, shirts, candy and chewing gum she had been able to squeeze into her luggage. In the first letter we received from her, she wrote:

"I know this is the day for the meeting of The Tom Dooley League [the auxiliary of our Chapter devoted to young members up to nineteen years]. I wish I could be there at this time to tell the students—Frank and Maureen especially—what I have seen in these past few days. If I could only put into words how very much it all is appreciated, we would have no trouble raising anything for the Tibetans. Here at Mussoorie, Peter and Susan are loved and respected . . . Tess, Dr. Dooley would have been so proud to see the mobile unit in action. The pitiful looks on the poor Tibetans, their complete trust in Vernell Geistweidt (the Foundation's nurse) and Dr. Chatturgee, the Indian doctor, were worth the whole trip."

The Tibetan mobile health unit, which was doing such a great job, was the first promise made by Dr. Dooley which The Foundation kept. As Tom's mother wrote in her book: "In November, 1960—two months before he died—my son had promised the Dalai Lama of Tibet two mobile health units for use among the helpless Tibetan refugees in northern India. This fine and gentle people, whose country has never in its history known war and whose religion abhors killing, live in misery and wretchedness because communist genocidal policies—including sterilization and castration—have made them flee Tibet in terror. This outrage against humanity is one about which my son felt most strongly. He, who supplied Medico with so much, gave his word that help would come, but this was a promise that Medico, after his death, seemed unable to keep. On January 17, 1962, Tom's birthday, the Foundation presented the two units to the Dalai Lama."*

One year after Tom's death and on Tom's birthday, Dr. Verne Chaney, Executive Director of the Foundation, presented the mobile health unit to the Central Relief Committee and the Dalai Lama for use in northern India among the refugee camps. The unit consisted of a van made in Oneonta, N.Y., and painted in the Tibetan colors

* *Promises to Keep*, by Agnes W. Dooley. New York: Farrar, Straus & Giroux, 1962, p. 256.

(orange and maroon). It was paid for by contributions from the American people, particularly those living in the Monterey peninsula of California and each donor signed the van. After the last signature was squeezed into place, a special coat of shellac was applied to preserve the signatures. The van has maintained its bright and shiny colors, because the Tibetan boys take such great pride in keeping it polished. The other unit, the jeep-trailer, contributed by the people of Chicago, usually takes off with its load of medicines into areas where the van cannot maneuver. Both vehicles proved to be a happy combination, as the two units were responsible for helping to bring relief and medicines to over 22,000 refugees living in the small tents erected in the camps. It was not uncommon to see the people line up along the road as the mobile unit approached the sick on its errand of mercy. As it lumbered past, it was affectionately touched by those on the roadside who either tied their prayer-scarves to the van or presented them to the doctor or nurse, as gestures of good-will and esteem.

When she reached New Delhi, Betty asked us to tell Elaine Reininger, a new and active volunteer, that Dr. Virginia Singleton was getting fan mail "like mad." Elaine had written a column in a New Jersey paper requesting readers to "Adopt a Doctor." Dr. Singleton, on a limited visitor's visa in India, was working on the van and in the clinic. She later left for Nepal and Khong Island, Laos.

Finally Betty reached the hospital Tom built in 1960, which is now staffed by the Foundation. It is located high on a knoll at Ban Houei Sai, a village located on the Mekong River on the Thailand-Laos border. On this memorable day she wrote: "Well, my dream has come true, and I'm at Ban Houei Sai. Dr. Dick Baldwin (a young doctor who had written and offered his help to Dr. Dooley while he was a student in school but was advised by Dr. Dooley to stay in school and get his medical degree first) is adored by the people, and if he didn't have to go into the Air Force I'm sure he could come closest to being what Dr. Dooley was to these people. He loves the hospital, the people, and feels we have a real need. He said the boat is the best for this area, which was good to hear." The floating hospital clinic had been donated by the New York City Chapter, and called the *Peggy E. Lee,* in honor of singer Peggy Lee, chairman of the Board of Directors of the Foundation. Its insignia is the Walt Disney character "Lady," and that of the jeep in the same area is "Tramp." The x-ray unit in Pakse is "Pluto" and the pick-up truck in Khong is "Dopey." Last summer "Pinocchio" was shipped for An Lac, Saigon, and our jeep in India is "Mickey Mouse."

Betty's letter continued: "I watched Dr. Baldwin remove a very large mole from the face of a 12-year old child. I also saw him treat a woman who had stepped on a landmine! There was a woman suffering from pneumonia whose heart had actually stopped that morning, and Dr. Baldwin massaged her heart and revived her. Another old woman hemorrhaged with T.B., and while I was there a wounded soldier was flown in." She then listed some of their needs: "The Mekong River is beautiful, but the hospital can be a lonely place. They could use a 16 mm sound projector and film, a good typewriter, any magazine subscriptions, and Dooley kits." Since this last item will often be mentioned, I had better describe a Dooley kit. It is a small cloth draw-string bag, usually made by volun-

7

teers who request a project. The kit contains a bar of soap, a face-cloth, a toothbrush, a comb, a tube of toothpaste, some tissue, a balloon, a small light toy, a lollypop and some socks. Each kit contains a message of affection, written in the language of the child.

"Tell Mrs. Nan Collins," Betty added, "to make the p.j. bottoms (requested by Mrs. Peg Conway, the nurse-wife of Dr. Conway, both of whom served in Ban Houei Sai), because so many patients leave the hospital wearing their pajamas and the supply is constantly running out. They also need wash-cloths and towels, knit bandages, different sizes of adhesive tape, $\frac{1}{2}''$, $1''$, and $2''$, ballpoint pens, bandage scissors, powdered soft-drink mixes, and our meeting notices."

Betty also gave us this glimpse of local native life: "A dear little girl, shy at first, took hold of my hand and led me through the village to her house. It was a thatched-roofed low building, but very clean. The family all slept and ate in one room, corn hung from the ceilings, and I could see the women doing some beautiful embroidery. We had to stoop to go through the door, then the child took me into another house and there we found Dr. Baldwin examining a young boy. This is where the river boat clinic can be of so much help. Gasoline for the boat and jeep costs about $25 a day. As we left, the people all stood on the banks and waved goodbye."

After her return to America, Betty Moul appeared on the Barry Farber radio show, as well as other television and radio programs. She talked about her trip to Viet Nam and Laos, and the response from the listeners was terrific. This inspired the New York City Chapter even further in its efforts to carry on Tom's work under the auspices of The Foundation.

Another notable volunteer is Edna Fannon, a young business executive working for Design 375. During the year 1964 Edna served as the president of the Chapter, and guided it through some turbulent waters. When Tom lived, Edna was in charge of assigning projects to those people who could not afford a monetary contribution but who wanted to help in some other way. Such people are always writing us, and we gratefully accept their help in any form they care to give it. It does not bother Edna to come to New York with a pail and scrub brush, for she is the one who spent her holiday cleaning up the office. Last summer, when we decided to solicit a few gallons of paint to brighten up our office, I had to smile when two well-dressed women, who had responded to the lecture Betty Moul gave at Teaneck's Holy Name Hospital, met me in the lobby of our building with paint brushes and gallons of paint dangling in coolie-like fashion from their arms. Said Mrs. Foley to me as she waited for Dr. Fox's wife to join us with her paint, "If anybody ever told me that I'd get all dressed up and come to New York and be seen on Fifth Avenue carrying gallons of paint, I'd never have believed them!"

To supplement the income that we realize from fund-raising events, the Chapter has also been selling cosmetic products. This source of income was introduced to the Chapter and administered first by Miss Mary Ann Whatley and Miss Marge Tuttie. Mary Ann was a volunteer who worked at Medico's office at 420 Lexington Avenue, and she answered mail from the doctors and nurses who volunteered their services. She worked with Tom's brother, Malcolm, and later for Dr. Emmanuel Voulgaropoulos when he returned from Cambodia and was assigned to the home office. Dr. Voulgaropoulos was one of the incorporators of the Foundation, and a member of the Board of Directors until he went to Viet Nam to work for the International Development Agency as a Public Health Officer in the central Highlands of Viet Nam. When Lydia Naas took over the cosmetic program in 1964, the sales continued to rise. This meant we had more money to send to the head office in San Francisco. The cosmetic firm usually awarded prizes for sales volume in the form of U.S. savings bonds and silver dishes, and these also helped our work as we awarded the silver as door prizes and converted the bonds to cash.

Younger people work in The Tom Dooley League in many useful ways. Some help us to pack shipments for overseas, and others keep the S & H green trading-stamps in order. (The Foundation had launched a drive to collect 21 million trading-stamps to purchase an airplane for use in our program in Nepal and Laos.) Several students collect the stamps and in their spare time put them into books. For example, Frank Schait makes a regular trip into New York City from Upper Montclair and turns in the books for redemption. We then send the cash to headquarters in San Francisco, earmarked for the funds being raised to buy the airplane. The young Leaguers also wrap bundles for us, prepare boxes for the hospitals, and make up the Dooley kits. They also solicit their friends for the various items needed for the kits. We are hoping that in time The Tom Dooley League will become a powerful tool for international understanding. It is a non-sectarian, nongovernmental and non-profit organization through which the very young can do something now, as they want to, and not have to wait until they reach adulthood. Many youngsters are so moved after reading Tom's books that they write us wonderful letters asking how they can help. We are happy to provide them, too, with this avenue of service.

I often wonder what Dr. Dooley would have thought of the office that now serves the Chapter in New York. He always had visions of a nice office, well run, with a minimum of expense. We certainly can boast of a minimum of expense, since no one is salaried and the room we occupy is called "unrentable space." Mr. Matthew Sweeney, the manager of the building, watches over us most carefully in his cheerful, warmhearted way. We have a million-dollar view of the Hudson River, some beautiful New York sunsets, and the office is always warm in the winter and cool in the summer.

Our office door is painted red. For some time the door caused me concern, because the molding seemed to be separating from the rest of the wood and it looked as if the office were being broken into. We put up new molding, painted it, and posted a sign saying, "This Office is staffed by Volunteers. If you wish further information, please call OR 9-0948." Not long after this repair job, we noticed we could see daylight through the cracks again, and for a while I was convinced that somebody had illusions of great wealth behind our red door. I was finally reassured to learn that the heat affected the wood this way. In any event, there is nothing valuable in our office—except hard work, which is priceless and always freely given.

When our Chapter first moved into the office, we formed

a Humility Committee whose job was to see that the desks were dusted and floor cleaned. Judy Rizzo and Mary Ann Sharkey attended to these chores, and I remember when Judy celebrated her 20th birthday, a sad farewell to her teens, by working among pill-bottles, leper bandages, toys, and reading matter. While her lovely orchid patiently hung on her coat in the closet, she and her teen-age friends hastened to get the place in shape for the new crew before they left for a more festive celebration of Judy's birthday.

In the New York City Chapter we never know from day to day what our problems will be. One day I had a call from a lawyer, representing a doctor's widow who wanted to donate all his surgical instruments to The Foundation. This equipment was delivered to New York while I was out of town, and when I returned I found my Metropolitan Life Insurance Company locker so full of the doctor's black bags and boxes that I could not get another thing in it. The next problem was to convey all this material to the Chapter's office, directly across Madison Square Park from the Metropolitan Life Insurance Company. We called upon Walter Connell, Tom's good friend, and he got a group of luncheon companions to form a "safari" for this purpose. After the stuff was moved, I asked Louise O'Connor Donohue, R.N. to come and look over the equipment to see if it was worth the expense of shipping to San Francisco. While Lou was on the floor examining the instruments in the many black bags, a knock came on the door. It was Dick Blanchefield, whose job in San Francisco had been to keep the warehouse in order. He was visiting his family on the east coast before leaving for Laos. When he saw the instruments, he fully approved the shipment and we were delighted to be able to send something really worthwhile out to headquarters.

Incidentally, Dick Blanchefield's story is worth telling here. He is an ex-Marine, age 27, who saw duty in Okinawa. He had majored in Southeast Asian history and had two years of college behind him. When he heard about The Thomas A. Dooley Foundation, he hitch-hiked to California to seek an interview with Dr. Verne Chaney, who talked to him and tested his sincerity by asking him to come back in three weeks. Not in the least discouraged, Dick took a job in a California hospital and a part-time job in a nearby orphanage. During the time he worked in The Foundation warehouse, he had written me: "I've never had any experience in anything of this type, but I know just where everything is. What's more, so does Dr. Chaney. I've got the warehouse separated into areas, and if you want a part for the jeep, or drugs, or instruments, I can find it right away." Dick later worked in Laos at the Ban Houei Sai Clinic and in Pakse, which is in southern Laos where we have an x-ray unit and then returned to complete his college course.

My greatest personal desire is to see the Tom Dooley Youth League expand and take shape. We hold meetings with young people three times a year in the fall, winter, and spring. Ted Torok, who was in Haiphong with Tom in the U.S. Navy, brought his films of Dr. Dooley to one such meeting. It seemed strange to see Tom looking so young and vital in these films, while the area of the world in which he had worked was still torn apart by the Four Horsemen of poverty, sickness, disease, and ignorance. I had brought to this meeting a copy of the medal that

Congress awarded Tom posthumously and President Kennedy presented to Mrs. Dooley in the summer of 1963. It was impressive to tell the students that the records of the U.S. Mint showed that the first such medal had been awarded to our first President, George Washington, while the last person to receive it—as of Washington's Birthday in the year 1964 (the day of our meeting)—was Dr. Tom Dooley.

Frank Schait chaired this meeting. He had grown a lot since the day he first came into our office with his father to discuss ways in which he could help our work. Frank had a wonderful idea at that time. It was so big, in fact, that I was inclined to think it impossible to bring off. I underestimated this teen-ager. His idea was to have the nationally famous Kingston Trio put on a benefit for The Foundation, and he felt he could fill the South Mountain Arena in his home state, New Jersey, with this drawing-card. Frank undertook this man-sized job on his own initiative. What is more, he first had to raise the initial down-payment on the Trio's contract, a matter of six thousand dollars, before he even sold a ticket! He went to work and persuaded some kind men in Jersey to put up part of the necessary total until he could repay them. The basement of Frank's house was then turned into a theatrical ticket-office, and his parents and his brother and sister pitched in. Frank, only fifteen at this time, was planning to be a doctor. He had become interested in Dr. Dooley's work when he read one of Tom's books which Mrs. Schait had received from her book club. His affair at the South Mountain Arena was a big financial and musical success, and he was able to send a substantial contribution to San Francisco. Frank, now a few years older and still a Kingston Trio fan, has entered his senior year in high school and has never let new interests dull his desire to continue Dr. Dooley's work.

The Catherine McAuley High School, of Brooklyn, N.Y., had sent young representatives to our Washington's Birthday meeting. Their school had dedicated their 1964 yearbook jointly to President Kennedy and Dr. Tom Dooley. Tom would have loved the fifth grade students of St. Catharine's in Glen Rock, New Jersey, who came to the city with their teacher, Miss Anne Sellers. All the class wanted to come, but Miss Sellers ran a contest and five students won the trip. Actually, *we* were the winners, as no prize could compare to the sight of these five eager youngsters who had sold pot-holders and presented us with two envelopes containing the results of their earnings.

During the meeting I noticed the starched bib of a nun in the doorway. Thinking she might be Sister Marie Julie, one of the teachers I was expecting, I made my way to the back of the room to invite her in and introduce her to the officers of the League and Chapter. She smiled and said she was not Sister Marie Julie and was merely waiting for her companion to join her. She told me that her community had been the recipient of a medal that Pope John XXIII had given to Dr. Dooley during his trip to Rome in May 1960. This darling Irish nun treated me as though I had been an assistant to St. Peter himself, and I exacted a promise from her to pray for the success of The League and our work.

Among those present at this meeting were twelve students from St. Mary's, Bridgeport, Conn. The name of this teacher, Sister Marie Julie, lingered in my mind, because it reminded me that I once had a teacher named Sister Julia, S.S.J., who had presented me with a portable typewriter when I graduated from grammar school. It had taken me a long time to master the typewriter, and I never dreamed I would spend so much time in front of one. Farthest from my thoughts was the idea that I would one day write a book! How did it all come about? How did I first learn about Dr. Dooley's work, and when did I come to know him personally? It all started nine years ago. . . .

———

Chapter II

IT STARTED AS "PEOPLE TO PEOPLE"

In the summer of 1956, while preparing for vacation, I packed away a new book entitled *Deliver Us from Evil* to take to the Catskills. I did not even know whether I'd have time to read it, and I would have been amazed if anyone had suggested that this book was destined to mark the end of my vacations and spare time for the next four years, and to change my life forever.

Deliver Us from Evil, Dr. Dooley's first book, was an account of his experience as a U.S. Navy doctor in Communist-controlled North Viet Nam, just after the fall of Dien Bien Phu. Dr. Dooley was ordered to set up huge refugee camps to care for the hundreds of thousands of escapees seeking a passage to freedom into South Viet Nam, under the terms of the Geneva peace treaty. Dr. Dooley, with the help of a handful of shipmates such as Norman M. Baker and Edward Maugre, managed to feed, clothe, temporarily house, and medically treat these leftovers from an eight-year war, before they were transferred to U.S. Navy ships and transported to the free area around

Saigon. By the time the job was done, Dr. Dooley was one of only four Americans in all of North Viet Nam, and he was the last to leave after the communists arrived at Haiphong to take over.

The book made a deep impression on me, and Dr. Dooley's vivid picture of the frightened refugees remained with me long after I closed the book. His sense of compassion, his deeply rooted faith, his patriotism, his ability to make you see the Vietnamese as real people and suffering human beings who needed help, made me re-read the book again and again. It seemed only right that I should let him know that I admired the work he had done, and his memorable account of it. So after Mass at St. Theresa's in Windham, N.Y., I sat on a bench outside the little church facing a mountain and wrote a letter to him. I sent it in care of the U.S. Navy Hospital at Bethesda, Maryland, where, according to the closing pages of the book, he had gone to recuperate after his return to America. My letter required no answer, and I did not expect one.

In the middle of the following January, while I was very busy typing year-end reports in my job as a secretary in the Metropolitan Life Insurance Company, at their Home Office on Madison Avenue, New York City, a strange-looking envelope appeared in my mail-basket. My eyes widened as I saw the multicolored, beautiful designs of the unfamiliar Laos stamps, and I wondered as I slit the envelope open what it could contain. There was a letter inside that read as follows:

It Started as "People to People"

c/o Carter de Paul
Navy 150, Box L
FPO San Francisco, Calif.
January 5, 1957

Dear Miss Gallagher:

Thank you very much for your very kind letter that you wrote to me outside of St. Theresa's Church many months ago. It has travelled half around the world to reach me here in Laos.

We have built a little hospital here, and with the same three men who were with me before we are trying to practice medicine and do some public relations for America.

Our little 25-hut hospital in the village of Vang Vieng is going strong. We see about 100 patients every morning at sick call, and after a lunch of C-rations (ugh) we pack up the jeep and two of us go into the surrounding mountains and visit the villages and tribes who cannot easily get to our hospital in Vang Vieng. When the sun sets on whatever village we are in, we show a movie. (Needless to say, *Bambi* has conquered Laos.) Then about 8 P.M. we return to our "capital village" and have a hot shower.

This hot shower the boys have constructed out of bamboo and an empty 60-gallon gasoline drum. It looks a bit like a Texas oil derrick, but it works well, and that is all that counts. A hot shower is a magnificent luxury for the end of the day. Never realized it more, though in the mountains the heat of the jungle is often crushing. The sickness and disease are a bitter and desolating experience. And everywhere there is that odor, peculiar to all of the Orient, in which the village, forests and fields make you think constantly of decomposition and death.

19

But the children smile, and the old folks have gratitude, and from all the misery of the putrid aspects of our job we do derive a gentle sense of satisfaction. Our work is not a long day's journey into the night, nor is it an overwhelming burden. We love it, and have that feeling of happiness that comes only when you have sought and found how to serve.

After C-rations for dinner again, we play the accordion, write letters, like this one, and hit the cots early. There are usually one to two night calls per night that we divide among us, and dawn starts the day again.

Many thanks for your letter, and please continue to remember us in your prayers.

Sincerely yours,
THOMAS A. DOOLEY, M.D.

I was surprised to learn from his own pen that Dr. Dooley had gone back to Asia. Naturally I had not fully understood the real significance behind those final lines of his book, quoted from Robert Frost's poem:

> *The woods are lovely, dark and deep*
> *But I have promises to keep,*
> *And miles to go before I sleep.*

They meant that Dr. Dooley had discovered his true vocation—to return to Asia to work as a doctor among his fellowmen without pay, without any recompense other than the satisfaction that comes from voluntary service. It later became known that while Dr. Dooley was recuperating in the Bethesda hospital, his family and friends had tried to persuade him to settle down to a lucrative medical practice and to get on with his post-graduate work. "How could I make them see that things would never be the same?" he wrote in his next book.* "I knew the promises I had to keep, I knew that the keeping of them would take me many miles back to Southeast Asia, to the very edge of tomorrow, where the future might be made—or lost."

Though the phrase, "the edge of tomorrow," appeared in the second sentence of his next letter to me, I had no idea at this time that it was so meaningful to him; I merely considered it a very interesting expression. Not only had I not expected an answer from Dr. Dooley at all, but I now realized that his answer had come from a country I knew nothing about. Laos—where was it exactly? I decided to find out all I could about this land, and to make it my business to tell the people in my company about his work. Since we were the largest insurance company in the world, I felt sure I could tell him he would have lots of volunteer help from among my co-workers. An additional help was the fact that Mr. F. W. Ecker, president of the Metropolitan Life Insurance Company at the time, was also chairman of the insurance committee of the People-to-People Program launched by President Eisenhower. I knew this program was close to Mr. Ecker's heart, and Dr. Dooley's work in Asia seemed to be an extension of it, and a means by which we could all work together. After some weeks of consultation with friends in the office, I finally sent off my second letter to Dr. Dooley. His reply came very quickly:

---

* *The Edge of Tomorrow,* by Thomas A. Dooley. New York: Farrar, Straus & Giroux, 1958, p. 3.

c/o Carter de Paul
Box L Navy 150
FPO San Francisco, Calif.
5 May, 1957

Dear Teresa:

I have just received yours of the 23d April in record time. I believe the mailmen of the world are truthfully emboldened by the motto, "Neither rain, nor hail, etc.," because in my case not only does a letter from Manhattan have to go half a world away, to the edge of tomorrow, but when it does arrive at that precarious point, it must then be loaded in a small Piper Cub type military liaison plane, flown four hours north of the capital of Laos, and dropped by parachute to my hospital compound. The pilot must be extremely careful of his navigation because Red China is less than five minutes' flying-time from my hospital.

You wrote to me of the People-to-People Program. Indeed it is a marvelous idea. If I didn't think so, then I sure as hell wouldn't be here in Laos. I believe that there is definitely a need in the world for American economic aid, but it so frequently doesn't reach down to the level of the villagers. They know this road, or that air-strip, or that water-pump was made with American aid, but that is a cold unemotional objective thing. I believe medicine is the best, or one of the best, weapons of foreign policy that we have. Here is the emotional, subjective personal touch. Here is one person talking to, working with, and perhaps growing to love, another person.

On a personal basis, we can make a sober honest effort to show our villagers, and the 15,000 surrounding people, just what four young Americans are like, how we live, how we work, and how we react. This is much more efficacious than a thousand propaganda leaflets. For example, here in Nam Tha the communists frequently make anti-American propaganda as they did in Haiphong. It depicts the American doctor with germs dripping like pus from the end of his hypodermic needle. This is looked at and frequently believed by a gentle, somewhat backward (yes, backward . . . don't fear the word) people. Then their baby, getting steadily worse with his smallpox, begins to die. They come to me, fearful and apprehensive, and they see the magic of my medicines. The personal compassion of my corpsmen blended with the potency of antibiotics gives birth to faith and, from the solid ground of faith, love and understanding can quickly grow.

There is a lot of hot speech in the world about "internationalism." But the word is meaningless unless one man goes to another nation, leaving his own, and tells a man of that nation about his own. This internationalism. There are many paternalistic muddleheaded men in the economic programs of the world (who believe themselves to be immaculately conceived) who are of the opinion that, where the economic standards are low, communism breeds. This is historically not true. My own hereditary land, Ireland, is one of the poorest in the world . . . yet hardly communistic. The richest, most Christian province of India, Cochin Tranvocore, is the one most controlled by the Indian communists. No, there is something else besides economy involved. We certainly don't want to go from one country to another promoting the the establishment of institutions which are beyond the capacity of the country to maintain. It must be simpler.

Yes, the President's People-to-People Program sounds great.

If thousands of individuals established individual contact with their counterparts around the world, a net would be built that would hold back the lies that the communists are burping out across the curtains . . .

On five occasions now I have written a sort of "form letter" telling of what is going on here, our life, our work, our problems, and the like. I send this to the IRC (International Rescue Committee) who, in turn, mail it to a long list of people who have shown interest in Dooley and in Laos. Though they have never gone on a money drive for me, they are my central contact point. I'm sure Mr. Angier Biddle Duke or Mr. MacAllister, the heads, would be delighted to send you anything you might need. And P.S. they've plenty of pictures of my hospital in Laos.

Regarding any specific aid, the old bugaboo "money" arises. I have about $7,000 left from my original start. I intended this to be but a six-months' mission, but some people sent me small amounts, my book royalties continue to come (that pays most of the cost here), and the Lao government is picking up a lot of tabs (like kerosene, internal travel, help, etc.). So I have made this a 12-months' mission.

I believe I can make that $7,000 stretch until the month of August or so. (Plane fare home for the three of us is about $2,500 alone.) I shall then return to America, write another book (*Reader's Digest* is also interested), then go on a lecture tour. The money the three of these make, plus what IRC can raise for me, will outfit me adequately to return to my beloved, though wet and infested, Nam Tha.

Do get the pictures of Laos and my letters from IRC—and push old *Deliver Us*. It is the sum total of the 52¢ in royalties that I get on each copy sold that keeps me in typewriter ribbons, medicines and food.

Again, many thinks for your personal interest in Dooley and his welfare, and write soon again.

Sincerely,

TOM DOOLEY

I sent this letter to Mr. Ecker, and he replied saying that he found Dr. Dooley's letter "extremely interesting." He also recommended it and the clippings on the Nam Tha hospital as "excellent material for use in some of our company publications in furtherance of the People-to-People Program." He added, "Apparently you have already started your own people-to-people program. It is exactly what Mr. Eisenhower hopes will be done on a broad scale." I felt very good about this. A secretary could really contribute something, even if it was only 52 cents in royalties by buying a copy of Dr. Dooley's book, to help furnish a shot of penicillin or to buy a new typewriter ribbon. Mr. Ecker's attitude and Dr. Dooley's gratitude spurred me on. I never could tolerate indifference and apathy. I now suddenly became aware of a great need in the world. Dr. Dooley's book and his letters not only taught me that there were far too many "have nots" in Southeast Asia, but they also showed me how dangerous this situation was to the peace of the world.

Deliver Us from Evil soon climbed to the top of the best-seller lists, and the longer it stayed there, the happier we all were. The waiting-list for the book in the Metropolitan's library grew every week, and additional copies had to be ordered. It was obvious that the more people were enabled to read Tom's book, library copies or otherwise, the more copies would be sold. I also felt it was important that people get to know about this work, and they could most readily become aware of it by reading his own account. It was around this time that we formed the Dr. Dooley Aid Club. We never thought of it as a fan club then or later. From the start, we felt our job was to get others interested in Dr. Dooley's *work,* and to help him and his work as much as we could. Actually, it was Mrs. Marilyn Faludi, of my company's publications division, who first suggested such a club. In the beginning I wondered what concrete help we could provide, outside of getting friends to buy copies of his book and encouraging them to sell *their* friends on the idea. At this time Marilyn took some pictures of the club members for our company magazine, and our "movement" was officially launched.

Dr. Dooley often mentioned how carefully his pilot had to navigate when they made air trips, because Red China was so close to his hospital. As things developed, I later thought to myself that if the Piper Cub bearing my original letter had made a mistake in navigation, it might have wound up in Peking, and life probably would have remained much calmer. A long letter came from Tom in mid-summer:

> Nam Tha, Haut Mekong
> Kingdom of Laos
> July 3, 1957

Dear T.G.,

When I read your latest letter I could visualize, in my mind's eye, the Metropolitan Life Insurance Company's building—wherever it is. I could see you running up and down the multi-decked place (don't know why I visualize so many floors, maybe it is because I haven't seen a two-story building for a year), passing letters back and forth, Marilyn Lanning (Faludi) Publications, Maryknollers, Texans, Jerry Leary, that fellow Mr. Ecker, Chet Fisher, and Buddha only knows who else. But I thoroughly enjoy it; don't stop.

I wish I could tell you just what time it is. I know it is July third, only because one of my Lao nurses told me that tomorrow was my Day of Independence. The air field is completely under water, so there is no telling when this letter will go out. I don't wear a watch. Don't own a clock. The people here do not lead a life strapped to the watches on their wrist. I cannot tell a patient to take her medicine at eight, twelve, four, and eight. I must point to the sky and say *"Ken cow sam, sui, lengh, mouvanny,"* which phonetically means take your medicine when the sun is there, there, there, and when the sun is gone.

It is especially pleasing to this "practical" thinking Irishman to read that you are so passionate about pushing *Deliver Us from Evil.* So many people write me and say they enjoyed the book, and they are "lending" it to all their friends. Curses on them! Even worse when they write, "I put my name on the public library waiting-list, so I could read it a second time." I'll never make enough royalties to buy antiseptics if that continues. Your underlining in red (should have been blue) the word "Bought" is delightful. Can't thank you enough.

You know, when planning this mission, at the same time I was on a lecture tour of the country, I thought how good it would be to have movies. Hedda Hopper gave a dinner party for me in that fantasia-land called Hollywood, and Walt Disney was there. That was my meat. By the time we went home (he drove me to the hotel), I had his promise of and now have a projector, sound track, small generator, and—to list a few of the films he gave us—*Bambi, Snow White, Fantasia, Popeye, Dumbo,* and about twenty others. We show a movie here every other night, to about a thousand villagers. We have hung a sheet up between two trees in the middle of the village square. This sheet is about the size of four double beds. The projector is on one side, the people sit on both sides. And what splendor there is in the eyes of the kids as they watch *Bambi* prance and sing!

Although some have seen the same movie four and five times, the crowd never seems to diminish either in size or in verve. And we never tire of showing it. The boys take turns, and I do too . . . being an expert at that 16 mm projector. But I always want to show *Fantasia,* while each of my two men has his favorites. This causes consternation.

One of the most difficult things at home seems to be to understand the heads and hearts of people here, on the edge of tomorrow. No matter how you try to point out to Americans that Asians cry and love, fear and hate, and react to the same stimuli the same way we do, you still hear the comments, "Well, the Asiatics can take it, they've always had poverty," or "The yellow horde can take more pain than white men," or "They are inscrutable, colder, more calculating," or "You can't trust a yellow man." And some comments get even more vicious.

Living in a village with them, being completely saturated with their life, their religion, their aches and pains, and joys and simple happinesses, yet still being an Irish American at heart and in my reasoning, I am thrust in a peculiar position. I have to explain some of the churlish world to my Asians, and when I return I am going to try to explain something of Nam Tha to America.

My people here are more dependent on other people, on the immense and savage sky, on the monsoon rain, on their animals and their fields. They live closer to the edge of starvation, closer to their land, closer to their own. They have many qualities that it would behoove New Yorkers to adopt. And strangely enough, aside from our technology, I am not so sure that Madison Avenue has any qualities that would especially behoove Laos.

There is neither immense desolation nor overpowering happiness here. The people walk as on a slender taut rope between the brutal earth and the rain-laden sky. If not enough rain, next year famine. If a nonproductive earth, next year famine. This strand is across the canyon between love and cruelty: the love for their own over the "frontier" of China, and their hatred for the cruelty they know exists there.

Even in their relations to me, their white witch doctor, they have conflict. They have been told again and again, they have been flooded with leaflets, depicting me as the American monster intent on experimentation, poisoning, conquest, and ultimate slavery. Why, even the flu epidemic which seems to be hitting all of us in Asia has been called *"Kia atomique,"* which means "Atomic Fever." Can they believe in me? Can they allow me to open the belly of their pregnant daughter to effect a Caesarean delivery? Sometimes they trust me. Frequently they don't. Many a patient on whom I have done a major surgical procedure is spirited away during the night, because the sorcerer in his village has proclaimed the hospital haunted, the moon not full enough, and the sky savage. It is hard for us to be tolerant. We would prefer to be a despot for the right, to impose my will on my sick, as I know it is the will of enlightenment—at least in medical matters.

Last week in the middle of the night I was awakened by the sound of machine guns. I thought (as I frequently do), "This is it. They've come to get good old Dooley." I wrapped my sarong around me (we wear what is called a *pakamo,* like you see in pictures of U Nu all the time), and ran into the hospital compound. There sitting on the front steps of the surgical ward were a group of Chinese boys throwing firecrackers in the air. The night was cloudy and the firecrackers lit up the mist. One of my interpreters, at my side (with a huge bolo knife), burst out laughing. I asked him what it was all about. THIS one was new to me. He said that the people were Kha Ko, a Chinese-Tibetan tribe, and that one of their people was a patient in my hospital. They were throwing firecrackers into the night's sky to frighten the devils of the air and the clouds away, that the moon might be free. The moon would help my medicines to heal their tribesman.

So life goes here. The teller of old tales, the legends of love and sweet grief, of despair and ecstasy amid the drums of death—all this lives side by side, in not too peaceful coexistence, with my electric lights, my otoscope, and my antibiotics. Do you wonder that ours is a life of tension?

Someone wrote, "East is East and West is West and never the twain shall meet, till earth and sky stand presently at God's great judgment seat." That guy was all wet. They've met, and we're in the middle of it.

My problems are at the infinitesimal level. Imagine the problems of government to government. Or perhaps they are only enlargements of mine . . .

The New York *Times* asked me to write an article for them on some ideas of solution of the East vs. West problems. I said I couldn't because I've no nifty global recipe for the problems of the world. However, I could and would like to tell their readers that vivid life can be maintained without the accustomed luxuries and comforts. Deep-freezes, subways, chrome plate, and air-conditioning are not really needed for a full life, and I am not talking like an esthetic missionary. (I like my blondes and bars just as much as the next . . . maybe a bit more). But I have discovered, here, that man's spirit can flame higher, and man himself feel far more noble in the execution of his life, if he finds a way to do better duty to his other man. We don't blather and bleat of the virtues of America, her flush toilets, the magnificence of Mount Vernon, or other praise-phrases. But we try to do a bit more than the ordinary in our duty to our fellow-man, and the people know we're Americans. Like that tired old cliché, our actions therefore speak louder than our words.

I have just noted that this is the third page. Excuse the wordy violence, but I type as fast as the thoughts come out (and sometimes as confused), and I've a lot to say. Living almost alone like this gives vent to wordy violence.

When I get back to America, I shall write a book about all this. It will probably fall from the printing presses with a dignified thud and languish on the bookstore shelves. But I have something to say—if I can only cage it in words.

My immediate plans are this, Teresa: in a few days we are leaving for a 19-day boat trip down from this underbelly of China to Thailand. We will go down through Nam Tha, then into the Mekong at Ban Houei Sai, on down to Vientiane. This takes around two and a half weeks. We have five *pirogues,* which look like large African dugouts. Can carry 500 kilos of medicines, so we will treat all the villages that huddle against the river. We can also show them three Americans, and most people in that area have never seen an individual with white skin. Then my two men leave for home and college. I will fly back in a small Piper (which can land in the strip, be it under water or not). I'll spend August and a bit of September alone; phasing out. I've a young doctor (Lao) who just graduated from the one-year medical school in Cambodia. There are two

Lao nurses here now to replace my men. When I leave, my hospital will be turned over to the government of Laos to become their third hospital. All my buildings, my equipment, my linens, my medicines—everything will stay. In this way, in departing perhaps we can leave behind us something more than footprints in the sands of time. The staff I've here, my nurses, midwives, corpsmen, village 4H-ers, etc. will, of course, stay in their villages. And I will leave, reluctantly.

After a short visit in Lambarene, at the invitation of Dr. Albert Schweitzer (French Equatorial Africa), I'll return to the States. Should be in New York by October. A month or two of writing, then in January I'll start a lecture tour for the IRC. The money from these three will be enough to outfit me again and let me return to Laos, to do it all over again. God and Irish willing! I hope sweet-smelling women and martinis don't dissuade me. That's about all for now. Thanks for all your interest, write soon again, faster at the above address . . . and keep praying like hell.

In another letter Tom wrote that summer he said, "I believe that in the village of Van Vieng we have in a very small way done what President Eisenhower exhorted all Americans to do; to help find a way by which the minds of men, the hopes of men, and the souls of men everywhere can move forward towards peace and happiness and well being. Our way is medicine." All of this made very good sense to me. I was more convinced than ever that in medical help Dr. Dooley had found a new key to international friendship and understanding, one that had never really been tried in the way he proposed to use it.

In this letter he also told us the story of little Ion, who was found in a heap of rags, burned black from his head to his buttocks with maggots feeding on the burned skin. He wrote, "But this I do know, we are indeed our brother's keeper. From the Fatherhood of God comes the Brotherhood of Man. And from the Brotherhood of Man comes the Community of Nations. So we are indeed our brother's keeper. It is not immature, muddleheaded idealism that proclaims this. Nor is it condescending, selfish charity. There is a simple, clearcut, vivid calling to those who have lived in freedom. This challenge, so flung, demands that we give to those who need some of our time, some of our humanity, some of our love, and some of whatever light we may have to give."

As a secretary, I asked myself again, what light could I really give? My only consolation was the thought of those royalties which Dr. Dooley's work received every time a copy of his book was sold. Every day after work a group of us would leave the office and stop off for an hour or so to avoid the subway rush. Over a cup of coffee at the Automat we talked about politics, vacations, hobbies, and of course about Dr. Tom Dooley. We wondered if he really would get to New York. We heard rumors about a movie to be based on *Deliver Us from Evil*. All sorts of accolades for him seemed to be developing, but one of the nicest tributes, according to everyone of us who read it that fall, was this letter from the Laotian Ambassador to the United States:

Washington, D.C.
October 14, 1957

Dear Dr. Thomas A. Dooley:

Upon your return to the United States from the Kingdom of Laos, where you have spent one whole year of hard work and personal sacrifice under the auspices of the International

Rescue Committee to provide medical services to the people of Laos, I felt it is my duty, as a Representative of my Government and my people in the United States, to say a few words of thanks and appreciation for all you have done to bring about health, understanding, and happiness in that part of the world.

May I be permitted to say in all sincerity, and with due respect and appreciation, that during the year that has successfully elapsed you have shown yourself to be a man of great courage, humility, and integrity as well as great personal charm. Your outstanding contribution to the well-being of the people of Laos marks you as a true American in the best traditions of your democracy. Your activities have been so extensive it would almost seem one lifetime could not encompass them all. Yet you have found the time and the energy to serve, to work, to lead and to help lead, shouldering countless burdens with unfailing patience and devotion.

In the course of your duties in Laos, you have earned, believe me, the esteem and respect of my people, esteem and respect you richly deserved. To me as to all my people, you represent the embodiment of what is good, righteous and admirable. The people of Laos, through this message of mine, is ever grateful to you for the public service you have performed with an unprecedented combination of tenacity, courage and devotion.

> Very sincerely yours,
> OUROT SOUVANNAVONG
> *Ambassador of Laos*

Chapter III

FIRST MEETING WITH DR. DOOLEY

I was working at my desk in the office on November 26, 1957, when the phone rang and a quick, incisive voice said: "Miss Gallagher, this is Dr. Tom Dooley." He was back from Asia and in New York. Before I could speak, he went on: "Can you get some of the girls together and meet me at sixish?"

I asked where he was in town, and we then agreed to meet at Connelly's restaurant because it was about midway between the International Rescue Committee's office and ours. I don't recall being too curious about meeting him, as I felt that I already knew him very well. I was really more concerned about the reaction of the other girls, and anxious that they would be willing to come to his assistance. His arrival at Connelly's one hour late didn't help my anxiety any, but when he finally showed up I soon saw that I need not have worried about the impression he would make. It took him about one second to charm the girls. He showed us photos of his hospital at Nam Tha and talked eloquently about his work. He spoke so intensely, vividly and at such length that many others in the restaurant, including the waiter, were also tuned in, although we were unaware of this. After Dr. Dooley left, we realized that people were staring at us. Some even came over to ask us who he was, and where they could hear him speak.

His manner of speaking was very fast, and not what most of us had expected from a midwesterner. We even thought we detected an Oriental intonation! But then I soon found out that he was having similar problems with our speech. Every time he came to New York thereafter, he made me pronounce the word "bottle" for him, and always laughed when I did. As a native New Yorker, I had a private chuckle in my turn over some of his words; for example, the word "merely" came out "merrily." That first day at Connelly's I thought to myself that it would be a tough job taking dictation from him, not because of his slight accent, but because he spoke so rapidly.

In connection with Mr. Ecker's People-to-People Program, Dr. Dooley was invited to speak to some employees of the Metropolitan. It was first proposed that he come to the office after five o'clock, but interest was so great that it was finally decided to give a luncheon in early December. The Dr. Dooley Aid Club—including Kathleen Kelly, Mary McInerney, Dorothy McCann, Madeline O'Brien, James Rieder, Mrs. Edward Distel, John O'Connor, Walter Connell and I—was on hand, of course. The heads of all the employee clubs were also there, as well as many officers of the company.

Dr. Dooley showed films of his work in northern Laos to this gathering of perhaps 100 people, who listened and watched with rapt attention. His narration was humorous, touching, and mercilessly blunt. He was warmly applauded at the end.

The next day Tom was called "Mr. Wonderful" on 23rd Street. I was very much concerned about reactions, and some of the comments I heard I have never forgotten: "He's no ham." "He's certainly not a phoney." "He's genuine, witty, and spiritual as well." "He's so Ivy Leaguish and so young to be doing so much." "He's a real go-getter, a born leader."

Little groups soon began collecting dimes and quarters and some healthy-looking green stuff to send to the IRC for Tom's work! We started to issue a little publication called *The Dr. Tom Dooley News Bulletin,* which contained items of interest from his letters, news of his appearances on TV, radio, lecture platforms, and so on. This little bulletin kept the bond of friendship so strong that, even after Tom died, the members never let up on their support, much to my amazement and gratitude.

By January, 1958, Tom was busy raising funds, interviewing potential corpsmen for his return to Laos, and looking for a man to help keep the home-front organized. He had also begun writing his second book, *The Edge of Tomorrow,* an account of his first year at the Nam Tha hospital.

I received an invitation from Mr. Angier Biddle Duke, president of the International Rescue Committee, to attend a dinner at the River Club to honor Dr. Dooley on February 4th. "A minimum of formality and no fund-raising" were promised and we were told that the young men who served with Tom in Laos would also attend. On this occasion Dr. Dooley once again captivated his audience. People always seemed to have a wonderful time when he was around. Part of the secret I think was that we all felt we had an interest in common—Tom's work and its importance to our country and to the world. This feeling of oneness made it possible for me to speak with ease to an Ambassador, a company president, or any stranger, because I was speaking for a cause and not for myself.

It was on this evening that the birth of Medico was to be announced. I can still see an excited Tom sitting at a table in Connelly's with a long yellow pad, preparing for the meeting of the Board which would decide if IRC would officially adopt Tom's dream. At a press conference Mr. Duke emphasized that "the medical aid will be given on a direct, people-to-people basis on the village level, patterned after the Lao hospital of Dr. Dooley and the work of Dr. Seagrave. Medico derives its inspiration from the philosophy of Dr. Albert Schweitzer." Tom promised that American medicine would benefit from this work. "Many of our young doctors will have a unique opportunity to study at first hand many of the diseases like smallpox, yaws, and beri beri which they study in medical school, but seldom see in actual practice," he said. Thus it was on February 4, 1958 that the new word "Medico" appeared. It was a word I was to hear many times before Tom lost the power of speech. How sad he became in those last weeks before his death three years later, because he felt that the child he had fathered had strayed from his principles.

The occasion at the River Club was honored by this telegram from Dr. Albert Schweitzer: "We send you from Lambarene our best wishes on the occasion of the meeting honoring you and announcing the formation of Medico, with which we are privileged to be associated." It was signed Pelir Albert Schweitzer. The doctor had broken a precedent in accepting honorary membership on the National Advisory Council; he had never before given his name to any movement. It was a great tribute to Tom. Adding further honor to the event, Ambassador Ourot Souvannavong of Laos was present.

After the dinner a group of us found a spot to have coffee. Dr. Dan Snively, medical director of Mead Johnson, Indiana, and Dr. Dooley's young co-workers—Pete Kessey, Bob Waters, John DeVitry, Dennis Shepard, and Norman Baker—were all on hand. They were in New York preparing for an interview on Dave Garroway's "Today" show. They had to report at seven o'clock in the morning, and Tom didn't let anybody forget it. Tom had so many irons in the fire, and he seemed to have endless energy. I found myself beginning to pray for his health and his humility. A few days later I sent a letter to Dr. Dooley's mother, Mrs. Agnes Dooley, telling her all about the event at the River Club which she had been unable to attend. It was the first of many letters to go between New York and St. Louis.

At the Metropolitan Life's luncheon, Dr. Dooley's film had shown youngsters wearing bracelets sent to them by his friends in America. He said the children loved getting glittering bits of costume jewelry in return for small jobs performed around the hospital compound. That was all we had to hear, and now jewelry was arriving at 23rd Street in envelopes, little boxes, and big boxes, and I kept packing it into a newly christened "Dooley locker," until we had time to sort it out. Years later Mrs. Peter Comanduras, visiting in Laos, was amazed to see Lao girls in elaborate hair-styles graced by beautiful pieces of costume jewelry from America.

Tom had another request. Could we raise money to obtain wooden boxes in which to ship some drugs and all that jewelry? These boxes were eventually to be used as furniture in the hospital. Tom explained his plan to cover each lid with linoleum so we had each box made with the lid on hinges. In the Laos hospital Tom sat on the box to examine a youngster and if he cried, Tom would hop up and reach into the box, pulling out a distracting piece of jewelry. In the beginning, he tried letting the kids pick out jewelry for themselves, but they got so fascinated with selecting that it delayed sick-call. He also told us that when the hospital was being built, the children brought bricks and bamboo they had "found." Tom was sometimes highly suspicious of the source, but the kids received payment for their supplies and the payment was our jewelry.

By February 1958 the drugs, medicines, and equipment that Tom had collected in America reached a value of some $500,000. Barbara Cox wrote in her column in the Los Angeles *Times* that Tom was a "highly eligible bachelor with a confessed envy of friends who have a convertible and a few girl friends." It is true that Tom declined the title of "missionary" doctor; he felt it did not become the nature of his work. Tom was aware that the honors and titles he had received imposed great responsibility, but he had a horror of being passed off as something he was not. Later, during his illness, when some mail arrived at Memorial Hospital addressed to "Dr. Tom Dooley, A Saint," he practically had a wild fit.

Tom seemed happiest when he was talking to young people. I often wondered how he could give speech after speech and not get tired of it all. By the end of a lecture tour Tom sometimes developed little blisters on the end of his tongue, and he had to apply medication. The secret of his success was that he believed in what he was doing. He had seen misery and knew he could do something about it.

Dr. Dooley was gifted in so many ways—as author, lecturer, pianist, doctor. Each of these gifts require very special talents, and Tom used these God-given talents to the utmost. Dr. Harold Blake Walker, Minister of the First Presbyterian Church of Evanston, Illinois, put it beautifully when he said: "Most of us never discover the full potential of our lives. Dr. Dooley was dedicated to a duty that *lured* the powers of his mind and body to the surface."

There were, of course, those who thought there had to be an "angle," and suspected Tom of being a self-seeker, publicity-seeker, and worse. On the surface they saw Tom giving lectures, appearing on television, or having his picture in the newspapers. Unknown, or ignored, were the facts below the surface—the days and nights Tom toiled as writer, painter, carpenter, plumber and surgeon in the jungles of Laos. Tom had to work very hard as the chief fund-raiser, as author, negotiator, liaison-man, and as doctor. He figured that we were living in a time when international communications had been brought to their highest development. He felt it was wrong to hide your light under a bushel if it could be sped to the far corners of the globe, and if from that light more light could be erected. He believed in Dr. Schweitzer's advice: "All that is necessary is that you make your fellow-Americans *aware,* and their awareness will act." While he had the utmost respect for the few doctors who retired anonymously to remote areas of the world to help others, Tom was convinced that the multitudes of sick and "have-nots" in underdeveloped nations required the help of multitudes of "haves." If the latter could only be reached by publicity, Tom was ready to go to great lengths to reach them. It is not surprising that in so doing, he encountered critics who chose to question his motives.

When queried about his work, Tom said, "We're ordinary people trying to do an extraordinary job in Asia. Without foreign medical aid programs, these villages and subsequently these nations will die." Tom described our ordinary government medical programs as "more dollar-to-person than person-to-person." To his way of thinking, the correct program was that you lived in the village like everybody else—even if that meant in a hut on sticks.

"You learned their language, ate their food," he once explained. "You went to the weddings and funerals. You became a member of the village council and, like everyone else, an intimate part of village life. One man is the blacksmith, another man makes clothes; I run the hospital." When Tom was asked if "this degree of intimacy was necessary," he replied, "Yes, this way you don't stand on a magnificent pedestal and reach down to pull the 'dirty' Asian up. You get off your pedestal, take off your gray-flannel suit, get knee-deep in the mud, and you push them up."

When he was asked, "Have you ever thought of asking the government for help?" he replied, "No, and I never will. America was made great by men who went out and hustled. They didn't turn to their government and say, 'Give me this, give me that.' In this era, all we do is turn to the government to solve our problems. It's not the government's business. It's *my* business. It's *your* business." And to another question, "How far can one man go in this huge area you've carved out for yourself?" Tom answered, "A man can go just as far as he wants to go. Four years ago this idea was a crazy dream in the back of my head and other people's heads. Now we'll have six medical teams working in Asia. A few years from now it may be 18, so don't tell me one man can't get things done. If every guy tries to do what we try to do, we can splash medicine and brotherhood all around the world." Tom's idea was that every man could do something if he got out and hustled and appealed to others.

Many people go through life unable to do something for others, even though they wish to. In our work we often come across people whose hearts are bigger than their frames. Tom discovered many of these people, because he had the key to their hearts. They were willing to give to Tom Dooley, because he was so willing to give of himself, and their offers of help came to him from all over the world. These people didn't have to leave home or abandon local responsibility in order to be of help; he provided a channel of service for them right at home. We grew to love many of these people without personal meetings at all. Mrs. H. Bellinger, of Magnolia Springs, New York, was a gracious lady who sent us a check for $1,000 every few months. These checks remained constant through the early days of The Thomas A. Dooley Foundation. Miss May Buckley, of Brooklyn, New York, was one of Tom's most constant benefactors. Although she was on a small pension, May sent him a contribution every month until the day she died. We felt sad when we recently lost both these beloved ladies through their deaths, not because their contributions stopped but because something good was lost to the world. Although our friendship with them was indirect, it was very deep and their passing grieved us. In early March 1958 *Life* magazine went to St. Louis to do a picture story on Dr. Dooley. Assisting Tom in making his work better known was Bob Hyland of Station KMOX there. Mrs. Dooley wrote and told me that KMOX and *Life* had laid so many cables in the apartment occupied by Tom and herself that it resembled the bottom of the Atlantic Ocean.

Somewhere along the way I got the notion that Mrs. Dooley came from Ireland, but Tom's family life and my own were something that we never discussed. Now Mrs. Dooley told me that it was Tom's grandfather who had come to America from Ireland. I also learned that Mrs. Dooley came from old Virginia and Pennsylvania stock. Her maiden name was Wise, one of her ancestors had been a soldier in Washington's army, and her grandfather had fought as a Union Captain in the Civil War. Tom's father's side was all Irish from Limerick County. As Mrs. Dooley wrote me, "Tom's genes are definitely Irish. He looks and moves and acts as his father and grandfather Dooley did, but every once in a while his calm, almost cold, American executive and business judgment amazes people, so unprofessional and not quite Irish. He has courage, stamina, and sentiment, a mixture of his heritage."

When the *Life* story hit the newsstands, the pictures gave me a more factual impression of Tom's lovely home and of his mother. It made me realize he was willing to give up so much. He had exquisite taste, particularly in jewelry, and often said that if he ever had a wife she would look like a Christmas tree with the jewelry he would always be buying her. He always complimented a pretty girl, liked nice clothes, good taste and grooming in dress, and made quick, keen observations about people's appearances.

By this time my 1950 Hudson was celebrating its eighth birthday, and it was beginning to smell more and more like a drugstore. The reason for this is that Sister Mary William and Sister Mary Joseph, Nursing Sisters of the Sick Poor, often telephoned me to pick up the drug samples they had been collecting for Tom's work. When I arrived, they would empty the contents of the garage into my car, and I would spend hours with my sister, Agnes McDonough, trying to sort out the drugs. This job furthered my admiration for Mrs. Auberlin in Detroit, who single-handedly set up her own drug center from a collection of drug samples. Her organization became known as World Medical Relief, and I often wish other ladies would take on such a project here on the east coast. Missionaries and doctors of all faiths continue to turn to Mrs. Auberlin for her aid. If she has the medicine or ointment they need, she reaches up to her shelves and sends it to them at no cost.

On May 20, 1958, Angier Biddle Duke and publisher Roger Straus held a coming-out party for Dr. Dooley's book, *The Edge of Tomorrow,* at the Harvard Club. When I arrived, Tom was enumerating the many blessings of the week. He said he had received one, a jeep; two, an airplane; three, an air travel card from George Skakel, of the Great Lakes Carbon Company that would take him any place at any time by air; and four, ten cases of Lipton soup. Speaking of the latter, one day I found Tom in his little cubby-hole of an office poring over some food catalogues. He was wondering how he could obtain some food that would be a little more palatable than the C-rations he and his team had lived on for so long. We talked it over, and I volunteered to write to the chairman of the board of Lipton's to see if anything could be done. Not too long afterwards I was thrilled to be able to tell Tom that Lipton's had made a one-time exception, sending him ten cases of soup *gratis*.

I soon began to notice that, when Tom was in town, things became much more hectic. Tom usually prefaced his phone calls, after the initial hello, with, "Can you get the girls together and meet me around sixish?"

We were always surprised to hear his voice on the phone. The better known he became, the more surprised we were that he continued to keep in touch with us. At our meetings, while I was unsuspectingly engaged in conversation, he would be busy figuring, planning, and organizing things in his head. Suddenly he would hit me with a hundred new ideas of things to be done. He always could out-think everybody. I also noticed that we were getting more involved with his work the longer he stayed in America. Kay Kelly jokingly said at that time, "I'll help you write a book, and we'll call it *From 23rd Street to Laos*."

On June 5th I took some vacation time and went to a warehouse in downtown Manhattan where Tom had stored supplies for his next trip to Asia. He was looking around to see what should be shipped, and I tried to be of some help. The warehouse was piled so high with boxes that it looked like an obstacle course. When Tom pointed out a container of one million aspirins, I felt I could use a few. I remember that sixteen boxes were already crated for the trip up the Mekong River. Tom then discovered that

Thomas A. Dooley, Jr. as a
Notre Dame Undergraduate.

As a Lieutenant, U.S. Naval
Reserve, Medical Corps.

Viet Nam refugees on a U.S. Navy transport, 1954.

OPPOSITE:

Above: The clinic at Muong Sing, Laos.

Below: Dr. Dooley in 1956 with Prince Phetserath, uncle of the King of Laos.

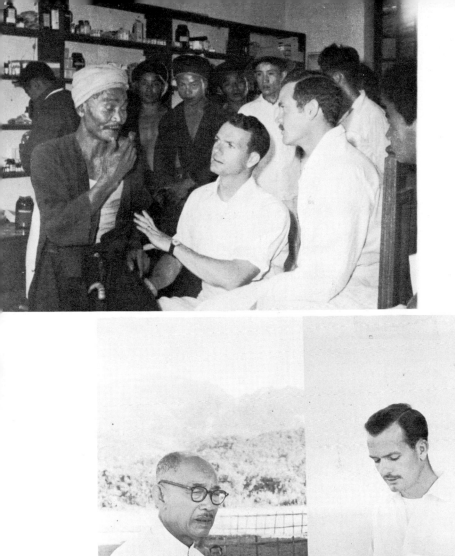

Above: In the U. S. with schoolchildren.

Opposite: With Lao children.

Opposite: President Eisenhower, Cardinal Montini (later Pope Paul VI), Father Hesburgh and Dr. Dooley at Notre Dame.

Left: In Rome Dr. Dooley is invested as a member of the Order of Mary Immaculate.

Below: The Lao Clinic, showing the O.M.I. crucifix on the wall.

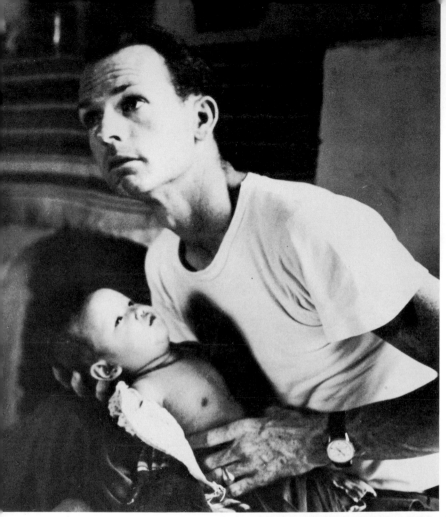

With a dying baby.

Ngoan at Dr.
Dooley's grave.

some of the hemostats ready for shipment were defective so he called Louise O'Connor, R.N., to help him sort out the good from the bad. Lou brought a team of nurses with her, and then finished off this essential job for Tom.

As the time drew near for Tom to appear on the Jack Paar television show, he told me he needed a blue shirt and a new belt. The two of us started uptown in the direction of Abercrombie and Fitch, to see his old friend Ed Shade. Tom was sporting a silver-colored mesh belt that had previously been wrapped about the waist of an elevator operator at IRC. One day in the elevator Tom admired it, and the operator had generously taken it off and swapped it for Tom's belt. Now that the mesh belt was tarnished, Tom needed a replacement. Abercrombie's was closed, to our disappointment, so we found another haber-dasher nearby. I looked around for belts while Tom selected the shirt. While I was deeply engrossed in making a choice among ten-dollar belts, I suddenly heard a blast from Tom that was loud enough to wake the whole Navy:

"What are you doing, Tess? Here, these belts are only a buck; they're good enough!" He then proceeded to go into an act that only he could dream up. He slipped off the old belt and nervously stalked around the store first in one direction and then another, loudly "worrying" about his falling trousers. I looked around to see if any customers were aware of his antics, and also for a place to hide. I hurriedly bought the first one-dollar belt I could find and handed it to Tom. He left the old belt on the counter and I put it in my bag and made a mental note to find out if it could be reconditioned. Later I sent the mesh belt to Tom all nice and silvery again. Once, when somebody wrote in and asked Tom for some personal piece of clothing, I suggested that he send that old belt, but Tom wouldn't hear of it.

It was almost time for Tom to leave again for the valleys of Laos. While he loved the country of Asia very much, he knew his constant companion there would be loneliness. Once he said, "I find it easier to see God in the jungles and to know God a little better. Perhaps it is the solitude." These days I often refer to this statement of Tom's when I speak about his work. In *The Edge of Tomorrow* Tom wrote, "In college we were taught the ubiquity of God. But to see God in all things when you are plunged into bleating materialism is sometimes hard. I certainly cannot see God when I look at a Mercedes Benz convertible. But in the jungle it is easier. Here we can know God a little better. We ought to shut up a few minutes and seek Him."

Tom left New York City by plane on June 23, 1958. It was a day to remember. He called us his "graces" and he had invited us all to meet him for breakfast early that Sunday morning. Tom's plans for the morning also included an interview with young doctor, Emmanuel Voulgaropoulos (called Dr. Manny by his friends), who had offered his services to Tom. The setting was the quiet, staid, upholstered main lobby of the Waldorf-Astoria. Dr. Manny was seated in a comfortable chair, anticipating his interview with Dr. Dooley. Kay Kelly was seated nearby, anticipating her breakfast. Agnes McShane was busy making phone calls to find a restaurant open at that hour of the day. Tom, who had just checked out of the hotel, was making an unexpected date to see an old Navy buddy, and bounced out of the phone booth with this announcement:

"Everybody up. Everybody up!"

"Where are we going?" Kay Kelly asked.

"To have breakfast."

"Where?"

"84th St."

"What's there?"

"Sy Spengler's."

"I never heard of any such restaurant."

Two taxicabs were required to accommodate us and our farewell gifts, which included a pillow emblazoned "Route 66." While Dr. Manny and Tom chatted imperturbably over the din, I got the distinct impression that breakfast was the last item on Tom's mind.

At Sy's apartment Tom rang the doorbell, and we all tumbled in. According to the clock, it was now lunchtime, and our host served us cocktails. "It figures," said Kay, who disliked confusion but found herself increasingly immersed in it when Tom was on the scene.

At the airport there was the usual amount of picture-taking, but finally Tom had caught his plane, Dr. Manny had had his interview, and we had had our breakfast—at four o'clock in the afternoon. As we ate spaghetti, we resolved that it would be a snowy day in July when we again accepted a breakfast invitation from Tom Dooley.

After lecturing in Hawaii, Manila, and Tokyo, Tom arrived in Laos on July 21. In the "Dear All of You" letter he sent us, we hardly recognized ourselves as the "great, good, glorious, sweet, kind, and gentle" people he called us. Tom said that the feathered hat I wore to the airport reminded him of a witch-doctor's hat. It was quite the style that year, and he said he was sure he could recognize it from 10,000 feet up, so I promised to wear it to the airport on his return.

Chapter IV

THE KELLY-GREEN SECRET

After Tom's arrival in Asia, he wrote us a long and detailed description of the initial difficulties involved in setting up a new clinic at Muong Sing:

"In Asia you absolutely have to 'fight' to do good. There are the terrible obstacles of petty animosities, jealousies, fear, mistrust, remembrance of white men in the past who weren't so good, communist infiltration, and many other hurdles. You can imagine the reluctance that the mayor of a small town in Iowa might have to massive Buddhist temples and hospitals and schools being built in the middle of his village. Well, this is not unlike Asia's fear of certain American programs. And it is really difficult for them to believe fully that I am *not* a Jesuit in disguise, *not* out to make an imperialistic colony of them, *not* a member of the C. I. A., etc."

He described his drive with his two volunteer corpsmen, Dwight and Earl, from Saigon to Bangkok: "Got the jeep out of Customs in a great hurry (unbelievably quick, only four hours, usually takes a foreigner about a week to get something out of Customs), and we drove from Saigon on to Phnom Penh, the capital of Cambodia. Had to drive through the part of the border where they are having a minor revolution, but no sweat. About a day later, we got to PP (as they call the capital here). In PP we stayed with the Ambassador, and pretty well sold our program to all the big-wigs in the Cambodian Government. It now depends on the approval of Prince Sihanouk, who is the real C.O. of PP. He has not yet okayed it, but we feel that he will, even though he is definitely anti-American, having just returned from a great and hospitable tour of Peking."

From Phnom Penh, Tom, Dwight, and Earl drove on to Ankor Wat. They spent the first midnight there "doing something I have done on each visit, swimming at midnight in the pool beside the court of the Leper King of the 12th century. It's a wonderful thrill for an old romantic like me." After two more days of muddy monsoon roads, flooded fields, several jeep breakdowns, drenching rains, and a journey across the Korat Delta of Southeast Asia (the prize that Red China so covets), they arrived at the capital of Thailand, Bangkok. Tom called it "poor billboard-battered Bangkok. The spot where East met the West with a clash." The kip rate of exchange had been lowered, and Tom's living costs were increased.

When he arrived at Vientiane and found some mail, it took some of his worries away. He planned to meet with the Lao ministers the next day. "Will they meet all my demands," he wondered. "Will they allow me to go to the area I wish to go, Muong Sing? If so, will they have enough gasoline, credit, and planes to transport my 30 tons of gear from Bangkok?" He ended his letter by saying, "I am fully aware of how many have helped me. I am indeed the hands; the heart is back home."

We soon learned that Tom's approach had succeeded, and permission to go to Muong Sing was granted. The Lao Ambassador told him: "Many times before white men have come to help us—but always they had other motives: colonization, trade, even our religious conversion. I really believe your motive is purely humanitarian. That will make your mission unique in my country. And, also for some of my people, a trifle hard to believe."

Meanwhile the Dr. Dooley Aid Club was expanding its efforts, and in the space of a few months we had collected everything from baby clothes to a can-opener that had to be fastened to the wall. The latter caused a sensation in Laos every time a can was opened, as it almost took down the hospital wall, and most of Tom's Lao staff wouldn't go near it.

When we weren't handling unusual requests from Tom and collecting, sorting, and mailing items to him, we tried to dream up humorous ideas which would give him a laugh. When a grass skirt and a lei arrived (which Tom had sent from Hawaii on the first leg of his trip back to Laos), we took pictures wearing his gifts, knowing how Tom's sense of humor would come bubbling to the surface when he saw them. We knew that with their tedious work and wearisome daily routine, something light and funny would always be appreciated, so we spent time looking for cards, books, and jokes. We had fun just imagining Tom's reaction, and we eagerly looked forward to reading about it in his letters.

In August we received a letter from Saigon in which Tom started his campaign to get us to "come over in a Boeing 707 Jet." He said he planned to have the children in Madame Ngai's orphanage meet us in Saigon, and in Laos he would arrange to have "an elephant or two on hand" for our arrival.

Mrs. Dooley wrote us at the same time referring to a "secret" that concerned me. It would be "interesting and gratifying," she said, and added that "you will hear about it before too long." I wondered if Tom could be planning to send me an elephant. It was not inconceivable, because when Tom was interning in Camp Pendleton, he rode around with a cigar-store Indian in his car, partly for kicks and partly to brighten things up for the R.N.'s. When Tom's brother Malcolm got married, the cigar-store Indian was one of the first "wedding presents" to arrive, leaving the bride with a rather perplexed opinion of her new brother-in-law. I wondered when the true nature of my "secret" would be revealed.

Tom wrote from Bangkok in September that the jeep trip back to Laos was a "gawd-awful thing, took two days and a night, and we broke a shock absorber, the tail gate, and our own behindsides. If it wasn't a road of mud, it was one of water, or a washboard one. Anyway we got the jeep and all the stuff to the river which divides Vientiane from north Thailand. Then we floated the gear across on small boats, leaving the jeep on the other side all night. We returned the next day and got it on the ferry-boat, hoping the jeep was in a state of grace, to say nothing of its state of mind, because that ferry-boat was not exactly what insurance people would call a 'good risk.' Now that the Lao government has approved Muong Sing, we are definitely going there.

"I flew back here to Bangkok, at the command of the King of Thailand, to be presented at court. It was most thrilling, and the King and Queen spoke of my work, had read both *Deliver Us from Evil* and *The Edge of Tomorrow*. Then the King told me that his father was in medical school in Boston when he was born. Imagine, the King of ancient Siam, born in Boston! The tonnage (now about 32) leaves by train in a few days. I'll fly back to Vientiane. We'll spend a few days uncrating certain things, and then 10 or so tons will be flown up on Lao Air Force planes (they have four) to Muong Sing. It is about a four-hour flight, across the staggeringly beautiful foothills of the Himalayas, to a plateau about 3 or 4,000 feet on the Burma-China border."

It was the next letter from Vientiane that unmasked the "secret":

"Dear All of You, I have just returned to Laos by plane this morning. It is afternoon now, but no one goes back to their offices until 4 P.M. because of the sizzling heat. This siesta is an international habit, and one that hyper-tonic, hyper-thyroid, hyper-kenetic, hyper-dooley cannot get into the habit of.

"Long ago I decided (after one wet evening at Connelly's) to name the jeep after my favorites, and my bestest backers. I could not get it painted at the factory nor in Saigon or Cambodia, but when we got to Bangkok I sent the vehicle to a paint shop to have TERESA, M. L. I. put on its kelly- (get that 'kelly,' Kelly?) green background. And the jeep jumps, bounces, and 'twitches,' so I think it is representative.

"Already we have been swamped with questions about the meaning of 'M.L.I.' I tell some that it means 'more love in store,' others, 'many live in sin' and finally, 'more ladies involved.' It means really 'Teresa and more ladies involved.' So you will follow us wherever we go, in fact, we can't get there without you.

"I had a week in Bangkok and was able to get all the gear loaded on the trans-Thailand train. It will arrive in Ngo Kai, on the other side of the Mekong from Vientiane, probably tomorrow. Then to the warehouse here, for sorting and uncrating. Seems like just yesterday that we were crating all that stuff. Remember? The field at Muong Sing is entirely under water, but I am flying up in a very small plane tomorrow for a look-see. The larger planes with the gear probably won't be able to get up there for a few more weeks. . . . but I'll find out. We are soooo anxious to get to work. The boys are spending several hours a day at Lao language lessons, and already can say such important phrases as 'where is the opera house' . . . 'turn off the television' and 'the gold is coming off the plumbing.'

"The political situation in Laos seems outwardly calm. One does not sense the urgency over the Quemoy Straits the way you can in Bangkok, or when reading the American press. However we are closer here than many others. Muong Sing, the village in which we shall work, is under martial law because of the terrorist raids, and the banditry taking place up there. All the more reason to get medicine and help to those who need it. There is an army battalion there, with only a male nurse, and other than that, nothing. The Prime Minister here has bent over backwards assuring me police and military protection, and I know I've the protection of Someone Else, a bit bigger than all of us. Therefore with that grace and the luck of the old Irish, I am not about to be thwarted. I can handle Muong Sing, and do a successful job of it, I am sure. But more on that village, after the trip tomorrow."

The Kelly-Green Secret

The two Texans with Tom, Dwight Davis and Earl Rhine, were to become very much a part of Tom's life, although he never suspected it when he first spoke to them. Mrs. Dooley was concerned over their wives back home, and she set about to build up their morale. She asked us to forward our Dr. Dooley Aid Club Bulletin, which by this time had a fair-sized circulation, and explained that she was well into her 19th scrapbook of clippings, concerning Tom's work.

"Dear Mesdemoiselles" began Tom's letter from Laos on October 5, 1958. He now admitted to being homesick and anxious "to see that witch-doctor hat," and he blamed his feelings on "foolish youth," dismissing it with "bah, humbug," and applying his favorite cure-all, "back to work." His letter continued:

"It is a slow Sunday afternoon, and I'm in Vientiane, the crew being in the north. The first DC-3 load flew up the other day. We skidded and splashed to a stop in a muddy landing strip . . . at least, on the map they call it a landing strip, though I personally think it was an empty rice-paddy. The gear was quickly unloaded by some fierce looking mountain people who are really gentle and eager to help . . . but they look like headhunters. While we went into the town so I could point out the things to be done the first week, the natives began to carry by hand some 4,500 lbs. of gear . . . some of the boxes weighing 200 lbs. each. (YOU remember, Teresa, don't you? Yes, I recall the warehouse very vividly and our lunch on the high stools on Grand Street.)

"The two sad, exhausted, collapsing earthen buildings that have been given to us were sitting in their respective buffalo wallows, looking absolutely disenchanted. Each building is about 60 feet long and 20-some feet wide. Each is divided into three rooms, and a tiny storeroom. One was the former dispensary, the other was the house of the nurse and his in-laws. All has been emptied out and given to us.

"The buildings are made out of this paste of lime, rice-straw, and water . . . with a little spittle added for its 'binding' qualities. After the sun dries it (not unlike Arizona adobe) it is painted with a whitewash made of lime and water. The roof is made of a type of thatch-tile which is constructed from tree bark. The buildings are low to the ground and have a small porch. Why they were not built on stilts, like EVERY other building in the village I'll never know. Each is literally in the bottom of a hole. There is a home-made brick walkway from the village road into the buildings. On each side of this walkway are buffalo wallows and a large village latrine. Staggeringly close to the latrine is our 'well' . . . which would be called a 'mud puddle' in America. The rice-straw plaster ceilings have all collapsed, water leaks through the roof in several spots, and the brick deck is a mess. Here is home. Here is our challenge! So the first plane load had cement, saws, lime, angle irons, screws, tools, masonite, tin sheeting, linoleum (to cover the top of tables, boxes, etc.) Clorox, Lysol, DDT . . . along with the Abercrombie Fitch camping gear, stove, a little food in cans . . . though not much yet . . . and that sweet surprise package from all of you to open in case of emergency.

"A plan of attack was laid . . . (no sense in putting the concrete deck down first . . . can't walk on it for 24 hours). I then went back to the airplane and flew out, leaving the boys in that little well of a valley on the very rim of Red hell. A rather uncanny feeling for them, I'm sure. Six months ago they wrote a letter; now they have been plumped into the valley, in a strip of land that plunges into the underbelly of Red godlessness. They had Si, Ngoan, Chai, Kam Lik, and others with them . . . but they do not speak Lao, nor French (Ngoan speaks English, sorta). They have never been in Laos before, and they are alone. And the night here falls unpremeditated.

"Tomorrow I will load another plane and fly up with it. I have to stay at this end because although the Lao Government is most willing to do EVERYTHING for us, they still need a certain amount of prodding . . . driving in bovine constipation called traffic here is difficult, especially at dawn . . . all are coming to the market . . . Then the plane is loaded and you wonder if your weights are exact, 'cause you are loading so darn much on . . . so close to the limit.

"The plane takes off and within ten minutes you plunge into the mountains over Van Vieng, and head towards Nam Tha. Hours later, flying over a cauldron-like jungle, mists, green, scarlet frangipani, trees arching towards God's heaven . . . the real forest primeval. Suddenly Nam Tha's valley sweeps clear before you. From there you angle a bit west and go up over the 'big ridge' some 9,000 feet high. Suddenly the valley of Muong Sing plops before you . . . from crest to crest only 31 kms . . . The plane has to circle lower and lower . . . maybe three times to lose enough altitude to land on the strip.

"Write again soon . . . much love to you all . . . give my regards to our favorite waiter at Connelly's (Gil Murtagh) . . . Wish I had some of those cheese things just now. *Koi mak chao!*"

Six days later Tom wrote again to share his life and

times with us. This letter was addressed to "Dear Ones," dated October 11th "down in the hot capital (temperature-wise, that is) . . .

"The buildings are all whitewashed now, and the place is really shaping up. Gosh the boys are fine. Doing a crackerjack job. We will really have a fine setup when you all come.

"TERESA is on loan to Operation Brotherhood, though I use it when in town. As soon as things shape up a bit with the government's monetary reform, they will have enough money to charter the antiquated Bristol to fly TERESA up to the north. She is too bulky for the small planes. She is really named for all of you.

"The north is looking fine, though the sick are overwhelming. We have to turn them away just now 'cause I don't dare start treating and throwing open the doors to hundreds until the hospital is fully stocked and ready to go. Otherwise we would be swamped and might lose a patient or two. Here, when you lose a patient, the people often get angry . . . and our job is dangerous enough."

Despite all the demands on his time, Tom still found time to write to us and to hundreds of others. To our surprise, his letter of the 11th was closely followed by one on the 23rd. He now had almost all their gear transported, and he was worn out from the "much gentle prodding, urging, gnawing, pushing, shoving, hollering, grabbing, etc." that accompanied the delivery of 32 tons of gear to Muong Sing.

He was still talking about our 707 Jet flight and he invited us to come out to Laos for "the trip of your lifetime." He said he was serious, but we were aghast at the idea. He tried to minimize our objections in advance—"so

you are in debt a few years . . . you will have seen Muong Sing"—but we were fearful of many other things
besides the cost: the thought of being captured by the
Chinese Reds, those large-sized rats and bats he described
so vividly, and the fact that with no other women at the
hospital the presence of single women might well cause
scandal.

Tom's letter continued: "I am back in Vientiane for
what I certainly hope and pray will be the last time for
many weeks. The transportation is definitely the hardest
thing to do. The Lao are willing to help me, and do . . . I
sent another ton up yesterday, and tomorrow (if the shipment from NYC arrives today as scheduled) I'll take that
ton up myself and stay on . . . The boys are doing such a
crackerjack job in the north. I've been up and back seven
times now, always spending a few days, but I hate to leave
to come back here. Two buildings are finished. The third
will start soon. Painting is over, well is being dug, and all
the other facets of a hospital . . . even to the new all-
brick bathroom."

Tom was pleased that we liked the idea of his calling the
jeep TERESA, M.L.I., and he announced that it had been
outfitted with a new compass by Mrs. Dooley. "She will be
flown up to the north in a few weeks, but there is some
discussion of parachuting her into our village, as the strip
might not hold the large transport needed. Imagine,
TERESA, M.L.I., falling from an Asian sky! The villagers will probably think it is a slightly front-heavy, kelly-
green hydrogen bomb. And I'll wager it will land on our
own 23rd Street (that is about all the streets in the whole
town—23).

"That's about all from this side of the world for just

now, *Except* that on opening various crates we found the wall can-opener, which is now installed. Si is delighted with it, but he pulls down some mud plaster each time he uses it, and Bau Penh Yanh. *Mou Koi mak chao li li.* Tom."

As Tom's hospital took shape and form, excerpts from his letters were printed in the *Dr. Dooley News Bulletin,* and in this way we shared his work with others. His next letter had two requests. One was for a turtle-neck sweater, (the shade requested, of course, was kelly-green) and the second was to "keep writing." We tried almost every store in New York for the sweater, but he couldn't have asked for a more difficult article to get. We even tried theatrical costumers, to no avail. After hearing a tourist describe her trip through Ireland and the lovely sweaters she had seen in Shannon, we turned in desperation to the Shannon Development Authority. A Miss Fitzgibbons answered our plea, and before long a turtle-neck sweater was flown to America, and it was forwarded to the jungles of Laos. While not exactly kelly-green, it *was* green, and since it came from Ireland, we dared Tom to complain about the color.

The end of October found Tom "in business" in Muong Sing and loving it, as he explained in a "Dear All of You" letter:

"What a help you've been! Louise O'Connor's instruments are in the autoclave at this very moment. A half dozen kids are sitting around on their haunches watching this bizarre group of white witch-doctors as we peck away at our magic instruments that produce printed words. And each kid has a 'Medico' tee-shirt on. Not a gift. They spent the day working, sanding pieces of wood, picking up scraps in the compound, and from time to time getting in the way, pleasantly so. Your boxes of costume jewelry are in a green (of course) chest on my left, and in the one I am sitting on. (No form-fit stenographic stools for us.)

"We held a hundred children spellbound this afternoon, by showing them a windup teddy-bear that drinks water.

"Our stomachs are in good condition. Our physiques are not gaunt. We are eating 'MLI' food. Sample medicines from the medical department, a nursing outline already being used as a model for our soon-to-be-started school. Every MLI contribution (and I mean EVERY) is being put to good use. We are sleeping on the floor . . . and it is a bit chilly these nights. Didn't realize how high these mountains were (that is a hint for a nice woolen turtleneck kelly-green long-sleeved sweater for Christmas). Sickcall is going full swing, but we stop at noon . . . starting at dawn, however. We look over the remaining crowds (maybe 30) and if any look desperately sick, we treat them. Otherwise we quit for lunch, then to work in constructing things. The local army is helping a lot. We have strung up a fine fence around the 200 x 80 yard compound, dug a deep ditch around the property too, and our outhouse has been built (green too I'll have you know) and more will go up soon for the patients. The Kha Kho tribes bring us the matting needed for ceiling and deck.

"We dug some lead out of an arm today. A man had tried to escape across the border at dawn . . . or just before it. They killed his two companions, getting him in the arm. He was in our hospital by early afternoon having walked down the mountain in that weakened condition. They are all very glad that there is medicine here. And they are grateful. So are we.

"There is much more to write about, but I'm a tired carpenter-physican right now, and had better go to bed, such as it is. For now, just one more request—keep writing."

Tom proved to be a very faithful correspondent, and we followed through with a letter as soon as possible, because we knew it meant so much to him. It kept him "in touch with the heart of it all," as he put it. In a cab in New York just prior to one of his last takeoffs for Laos, Tom went to a lot of trouble to tell me how much he enjoyed my letters. I remember how he often amused himself—and me—by deliberately misinterpreting what I wrote. On one occasion I described a reception at which a mutual friend of ours had sung. I then related that as we left the party, our exit was halted by a large cat squatted on the stairway. We nearly injured ourselves as we suddenly came upon the creature. I wrote, "I hope they have killed the cat by the time you get back here," and Tom replied, "That wasn't a nice way to talk about a friend who tried to entertain you."

Tom's descriptions of the living conditions of the typical Lao home were fascinating to us: "They do not use beds as such. Their houses are built on wooden platforms, or in certain tribes, over a mud floor. They walk on the floor with their dirty feet, but over in the corners they have a sort of platform, perhaps 15 feet long. This is about a foot off the floor and is usually covered with a bamboo matting. On this they sleep, sit, and visit and eat, though their cooking and the rest of the living is done on the real floor."

Tom's platform was about 16 feet wide and 18 feet deep. On it they laid down their mattresses, plus two "extra guest ones." He was becoming more and more insistent about our visiting Muong Sing ("and by damn, you *must* come"). He felt we would better understand the need for his program, if we actually saw the conditions with our own eyes. We also felt that Tom was so homesick that the prospect of seeing friends, whether or not they were scared to death, appealed to him. When we learned that Mrs. Bridget Flanigan returned safely from Laos, we had to admit if she survived, we probably could. But then we also heard tales of the French pilots drinking brandy and reading books *in flight*, so we didn't say yes to Tom, nor did we say no. His next letter included a copy of the "floor plans of the hospital," incorporating the cold brick floor of the outhouse, now christened UNCLE TOM'S CABIN.

Tom had asked us to make a call on his friend, Dr. Papanicolaou at the New York Medical Center, and I wrote describing the visit: "I decided to take along a box of jewelry and the file on you and I put both in a shopping bag. When we disembarked at 68th Street, I found myself on the platform without a bottom to the shopping bag. I had to carry it like a baby, and this is the way we entered Dr. Pap's office. We introduced ourselves, and he set about to make us comfortable.

"We showed him the box of jewelry as an example of the work being done, and told him about the kids and the bricks and bamboo poles. He threw back his head and laughed at the thought of the kids taking bricks from their own homes for you. We then went over the photos of the hospital and the main house, and pointed out the kitchen and shower area and main hall. When he wondered if you had it insulated against the heat, Kay proceeded to tell him all about the material in the buildings. She sounded like a construction engineer. He kind of surprised us by asking,

'Maybe you girls plan a trip to see Dr. Dooley?' We read him an excerpt of your idea on this matter, and we talked a little of it.

"When he asked us how we got the *Dr. Dooley Aid Club News Bulletin* together, we explained our procedures and he said he would like to be put on the mailing-list. He was pleased as punch that you had thought of him, and he thanked us profusely for coming up. When we asked permission to take some pictures, he had his wife come in and meet us, and she posed with us. I told her you had said some lovely things about her.

"Lou was thrilled at the opportunity to meet Dr. Pap, and is busy reading about the Pap smear test and his other work. Dr. Pap expressed the hope we could get the pictures to you for Christmas, and Kay said they will be ready tonight.

"Dr. Pap asked Kay to write our names down for him, and I guess he will be sending you a note of our visit. We left at about 6 P.M. and proceeded to board the subway sans bottom, of the bag that is, of the *shopping* bag that is."

I was privileged to meet with Dr. Papanicalou on later occasions, and the famous cancer specialist had ideas of his own on how to keep Dr. Dooley's memory alive. He felt that a free cancer clinic should be established in America, the money for the hospital being raised by public subscription and, he said, the government matching the fund. It was his thought that the American Cancer Society would staff and equip the hospital. Unfortunately, he never lived to see this fine idea become a reality.

Mr. and Mrs. Malcolm Dooley announced the arrival of Thomas Anthony Dooley, IV, just before Christmas, and

Emily Rhine expected her baby around the first of the year.

We had sent the wishbone of our Thanksgiving turkey to Tom; it was tied with a ribbon—green, of course. He answered with a long Christmas letter on "the morning of the night before Christmas," telling us that he had just had "Si and Ngoan break the wishbone, after much explaining about this bizarre American custom. They were like two little girls, giggling, laughing, and tugging. Ngoan won, but refuses to divulge his wish."

"Tonight being the night it is, I want to get this note off to you with all the sincerity I can muster. Want to say thanks for so much—the gifts, the paper, the money, yes . . . but mostly, thanks for thinking about Dooley, remembering him, loving him a little. Many people speak well to me and of me. They have a hot flash about my work, and forget it in a week. You have that constancy of the spirit that is the much needed Rx for such a world, and such a guy. Thanks. Thanks with all my heart."

Tom missed getting newspapers promptly, especially, he said, when a French pilot told him "President Eisenhower is in a satellite as big as a boxcar, wishing everyone Christmas cheer. What the divil???? We *must* get those newspapers." The Dooley Aid Club quickly sent him a subscription to the international edition of *The New York Times*. He also wrote:

"You know that any letter to Teresa is to all of you, onacounta I love you all ('tis safer that way too). The Monthly Payroll Team's Spiritual Bouquet was wonderful. Catholic is certainly *universal*, isn't it? North Nigeria, Africa, Europe, St. Patrick's, Laos . . . all around the world it is the same Mass, the same offering, the same 'I will go unto the altar of God, to God Who gives joy to my youth'.

"By the way, I've *the* sweater on now, and it is wonderful. I will get a picture in it, and send it on.

"Tomorrow we are spitting a piggy outside at high noon (Si will start on it about dawn). Sick call as usual, but at noon we'll eat the pig, with Borden's mashed potatoes, local cabbage, open three bottles of champagne that I bought in Hong Kong many months ago (drink it out of coffee cups), then eat with our seven student corpsmen, La, Panne, Dam, Deng, Hounpenh, Somoun, and Bountanh, plus the two nurses stationed here, Vong and Kham Ton, and our interpreters, Chai, Ngoan, and Savath, plus the three coolies, Leu, Lauh, and La, a visiting nurse from a village south of here, Earl, Dwight, and me. We have wrapped some little kind of a present for each one, and will explain Christmas to them. So far all they know is that we are having some sort of White Man American *baci*. Much love to you all, on Christmas eve and always."

Chapter V

THE JOY OF OUR WORK

From the high valley of Muong Sing at the foot of the Himalayas at two o'clock in the morning of January 20th, Tom started a letter to us—one of some two hundred, he said, waiting to be answered. A medical emergency at one A.M. had got him out of bed, and afterwards coffee had stimulated him to tackle the letter-writing job. He wrote that he considered it a "sin of omission" if he did not "reply to those grand people who write to me. I like to talk to people over this portable. Sometimes the joy of our work can fly far over the sea. This is better than to have it merely light up the silences of our soul." Tom continued, "A young man came in about eleven tonight with severe stomach cramps, so severe that I feared perforation of the gut. However, we were able to get enough of the right (donated) medicines into him to quiet the spasm, and at the moment he is resting quietly. No need for surgery, if he keeps quiet until tomorrow morning. Otherwise, we may spend the early dawn dripping ether and doing some more flashlight surgery.

"A regular run of hare lips and hernias this past week. The word is out that the American witch-doctor can cure those maladies well, so they come from all around the valley. The boys [his assistants] are full of anticipation for February 1st, when they go to Hong Kong for their first vacation. I don't know why they act so, I gave them a day off last year. Then I'll be alone, save for a visiting college lad from Boston who doesn't know a scalpel from a speculum, even though he does have a good heart and shares the family rosary with me. Total refugee count last month, 3800. Miserable, wretched, beaten, tired. How terrible it must be to be wrenched from your land like that. China keeps belching them out to us. Lincoln said that Americans should keep an ear 'tuned to the still sad song of humanity.' Here it thunders."

Tom, always great at thinking up projects, now told us he had a new one—a school. It involved 21 young students in the village of Ban Koun; their young teacher's name was Savath. The schoolhouse, Tom said, "looked like a, well, it defies description. It is simply a rectangle of rough hand-hewn wood with walls about 10 feet high. Then an open space. And supported above on a wooden frame is a thatch roof. The village has a great many lepers in it. It is on the China frontier, and I can walk to it in about two hours. The kids are very anxious to learn, and are bright and enchanting. They are proud, and can write the Lao language and read it pretty well. We have a 'vitamin program' there; each child takes Deca Vi Sol drops in the morning upon arrival at school (about 7 A.M.) and in the evening when they go home (about 5 P.M.). They understand the word 'germ,' here called *mehpinh vat,* and the importance of washing, though they have no soap."

Those four last words did it. Shortly after we read this letter, Mildred Kirschoff and Marie Muldoon, leaders of a group in the Dr. Dooley Aid Club, shipped out boxes of soap, blank books, rulers, crayons, and some sweaters, each of which was carefully packed in a plastic bag. It was not long before we received a thank-you note from the students in Savath's class. The original letter in Laotian looked like this:

and translated as follows:

Wednesday, June 10, 1959

Respected Doctor,

We, 21 schoolboys and girls of Ban Koum, are very happy to acknowledge receipt of your generous gifts such as pencils, rulers, cookies, toys, towels, bow-ties and shirts that you have so kindly sent to us. We are very grateful to you and feel too honored to keep these precious souvenirs.

Furthermore, may we pray all divinities throughout the Universe to safeguard forever your country and yourself.

Best greetings.

Marion Foley, another member of the Dr. Dooley Aid Club, sent Tom the wherewithal to set up a little photo lab. so he and his team could develop and print films and get the pictures out to their friends. Tom called it "Foley's Dark Room."

Even at this early stage, Tom's most loyal supporters were students. He was proud and grateful for their help and singled out, in particular, P. S. 182 in Brooklyn, and its principal, Mr. Israel Solemnick; St. Teresa of Avila, in South Ozone Park, L. I.; New Rochelle College; Academy of St. Aloysius in Jersey City, New Jersey; Franklin School No. 3 in Passaic, N.J.; St. Peter's College, Jersey City, N.J.; and St. Joseph's School in Bronxville, N.Y.

Tom first thought of Medico as a "baby," then a "sprite laddie," and at the age of one year a "mature gentleman." I was more inclined to think of it in terms of a sleeping giant, or as the expected baby that turned out to be quintuplets!

A three-page letter dated January 31, 1959, told us that our Christmas "cheer," noisemakers, pretzels, sheet-music and other gifts had arrived after New Year's. Tom said that Chai's wife was all decked out in the beaded sweater, and "everybody was grinning all over the place." No operations were scheduled because something was wrong with the electric generator, so Tom had hustled off for a hot shower. He always required his team to be clean-shaven and clean-shirted, and they never sat down to a meal in the clothes they worked in all day.

"The butchery continues, and it is terribly difficult to keep from getting complacent about it—as one does in the traffic accident emergency room of a hospital," he went on. "We just see *so* much—this decade's inhumanity to man." His thoughts turned to more peaceful things and he then mentioned the Capuchin Franciscan Church on 31st Street, which he called his "special New York City church. I go there on the way to Penn Station, and frequently when dashing around Manhattan. They have confessions all day long, and Masses start when I like to go to Mass . . . about 5 A.M. I loved the pictures of Dr. Pap. Seems you fulfilled this request with excellence (how else?). Many thanks, you are helping us more than you realize. He is a grand old gentleman, isn't he?"

When the two team members, Dwight and Earl, finally left for Hong Kong, "Si gave the boys a goodbye *baci*, and they loved it." Tom assured us that he liked the cards we sent "nasty ones, too, and I do love you all in my fashion (humor, humor, humor)."

Tillman Durdin, a newspaper correspondent, visited the hospital at Muong Sing around this time. Tom hopefully wrote: "I believe Durdin will write an article on us someday." And he did. On February 15, 1959, *The New York Times* carried an article under the heading AMERICAN IN LAOS RUNS SECOND HOSPITAL. It gave us much joy to see Tom's efforts recognized, especially because it would mean he would get more help. Tom's reaction was also joyous, and he said he was "delighted that he (Durdin) did not write about us in the same breath as the refugees, the KMT, and the border-fighting. We must remain above the politics, though immersed in the results." Soon afterwards

Tom learned that his new book, *The Edge of Tomorrow,* had been favorably reviewed by *The New York Times Book Review.* He was particularly pleased with this comment: "Through anecdote and an Irish gift for the felicitous phrase, he brings the reader an understanding of Laotian individuals, their ways of living, their attitudes, beliefs and superstitions—and their tragic needs, among them the need of simple, elementary medicine."

Tom had made a short documentary film of his work, with a sound track to accompany it. We used it for the first time at the Hanover Park Regional High School. We developed an informative map to go along with the presentation of the film, it was a real lesson in geography for many. The students were delighted to see Tom give a paper Santa Claus or a piece of costume jewelry to Lao children. We later learned that we had slightly misplaced the village of Muong Sing on the map! Tom's next letter consoled us with: "Don't feel bad putting Muong Sing too far to the East. Few know us. The mist is heavy here. But the refugees find the village, and find their morning here, too. Still gushing forth, the communes are a hideous thing thrown at the villager. The Asian, especially the Chinese, is the most dependent 'family' man in the world. The communes attack that very thing, the family, the tombs of their ancestors, the land of their forefathers. It is a 'reform' that the most simple people find repugnant.Villagers say that even the freedom to eat where and when they choose is now lost in the system of community mess halls. The beloved Chinese tea-houses are closing, but the people's dissatisfaction with the system is taking on a negative aspect—escape, rather than fight. The agony of China must be intense. A little of her blood splashes over on us here in Muong Sing."

In this letter, he called himself "a tired old man by the name of Dooley," and of course we did not take this seriously. It was not until six months later that he came home for his operation, and this was the first reference he made to being tired. I did not appreciate the significance of the letter until much later on. I was to hear him refer to himself as an "old man" many, many times before he died.

It had been a very busy period in the hospital, he explained. "The visiting surgeon did a lot of work with me, and helped me on tumors and the like that I would not risk doing alone. As a consequence, we have several post-operative cases in the ward requiring constant vigilance. We also had a hideous bear-mauling case and, yesterday afternoon, a blazing case of spinal meningitis with whom I spent most of the night. Then the plane brought in a liver abscess which has ruptured into the lung, and also a fulminating terminal tuberculosis. The ward is jammed, two in every bed. One patient sleeps in the dressing-room and during the day in the hallway. The meningitis case is sleeping in the clinic room today. In addition, Ngoan and Si have malaria and are bedded down for several days. Chai's wife is doing our cooking. Life *can* be beautiful.

"When you contact Father Keller (Maryknoll), mention that a thought for the day might be to remember in all the growing sophistication of today that most of the world is filled with simple people, the peasantry of Asia for example (her bone and her sinew). God must love these people because He made so many of them. It might behoove all of us to pray for them, not only for the final resting place of their immortality, but for the present resting place of their wracked and wretched bodies. We

75

might pray to learn the pharmacopoeia of brotherhood. We might pray that these frantic, frightened, sometimes foolish villagers will be able to find peace of body as well as peace of soul. Their hearts will only find their morning if their bodies live through the night." By this time, Tom's coffee had run out, his eyes were blinking, the fire was dead, the kerosene lamp was hissing, and it was now three A. M. He encouraged us to "keep up the good work for all of us."

When the crew members, Dwight and Earl, did not return by the 18th of February, Tom was very much concerned. They had been due in Vientiane on the 15th, and in Muong Sing on the 16th. Things were pretty hectic without them, and the loss of the only key to the jeep while the boys were away did not make life easier for Tom. At times like this, his Irish temper flared. In the hope of soothing his feelings, we rushed to him a copy of *Rice Roots,* a book he had requested earlier. We hoped he could get lost in the book, and that his problems would be forgotten for a few happy moments.

Tom wrote elatedly that the boys had *returned* on the 19th at noon! (More important than General MacArthur's promise, it seemed to me at the time.) They brought with them a new portable typewriter (green, of course), and Tom gave his old typewriter to Ngoan. Tom hated to part with it, for he had written his first two books on it, carried it through the evacuation of Viet Nam, flew around the world several times with it and, as he said, "Dr. Schweitzer's hand tapped on it with grizzly reverence as he told me, 'These machines do not give a man time to think, before they splash his thoughts on paper.' Now the old machine is gone to Ngoan,—so at least it is still in the family."

The Joy of Our Work

At Connelly's restaurant, our favorite waiter, especially when Tom was in town, was Gil Murtagh. One night Gil served three men, two of whom were carrying copies of Tom's book, *The Edge of Tomorrow*. Gil could not stand the suspense and finally had to inquire if they knew Tom Dooley. Indeed they did, and two of them planned to go to Laos! We thought it extraordinary that in a big city like New York three strange men should pick "our" restaurant, get served by "our" waiter, and turn out to be planning a visit to "our" Tom.

Martha Dean, of WOR radio, broadcast a tape Tom had made in Laos for her show, in which a little Lao youngster started off with a delightful greeting in English, "Good morning, Marsa Dean." The Dooley Aiders' job was to get the tape out of Customs and deliver it to Miss Dean. It cost us five dollars to do so.

For St. Patrick's Day we took a chance and put some Irish whiskey into some plastic shampoo bottles and tied green ribbon around them. There was one for each team member; we put their names on the bottles in nail polish. Later we got a letter from Tom saying that we were "an integral part of our day. Your shirts are being worn, your candies are being eaten, and your nips are being nipped."

Tom always managed to make us feel a vital part of his work, and every letter brought us a bit closer into the circle. We were not particularly aware of it at the time, but I found myself increasingly involved in his projects and in thinking of ways to help him. From Muong Sing in late March came more news.

"Dear All of You: Mail came today, two days late, like Pandora's box, full of little notes, scraps of paper, remarks

77

from Madeline calling me a 'scalawag' (whatever that is) and best of all the grand coffee mug with a green Santa Claus at this moment a-setting afore me doing what O'C [Tom's name for Walter Connell] meant for it to do . . . holding hot coffee). If any of you ever come to Muong Sing, now or in the next century, you will wonder how St. Patrick's Day became so well known here. After we read, smiled at and loved the St. Patrick's Day cards, we gave them to the children who have done a little work. (Ten minutes' picking up around the yard is enough to earn a prize.) They are thrilled. They loved seeing their photos in your *Home Office* magazine. I am NOT a monster, a Dickensian character exploiting child labor, but I am one who believes in pride—even the pride of small children. They are much happier when they 'earn' a balloon or a candy-bar than when one is 'given' to them. Also, they develop a feeling that the hospital is theirs. To further this, we have finished our playground, beside the ward, between it and the Waldorf Tower (outhouse). There is a swing, a jumping pit, broad and high, and some parallel bars. The kids are there constantly. The real sickened little lads lie on outdoor beds and can watch the others, and the others come and talk to them. Hence the sickened get better sooner.

"One P.M. next afternoon. We've some tragic cases in the hospital now . . . some interesting ones . . . some successful ones. Since we opened a bladder and removed a stone, the word has spread that we can help people with the symptomology associated with this. As a consequence, we have been cutting stones out constantly. The largest stone weighed a little under two ounces, the size of a duck's egg, a big one.

"We also have a little Kha Kho boy named Guntar, who

was mauled by a tiger. He is about seven years old, and his whole left leg is just one mass of torn flesh, scar and pus. This happened six weeks ago, but the lad's family couldn't get him out of China until the other day. He was absolutely the filthiest child I have ever seen. We spent a good hour scrubbing him up. Have a lot of pictures of him now that he is clean . . . and he's a charmer. He is desperately afraid however. If his father leaves him a moment, he lets out with piteous, animal-like wails. He is getting better, though. Right now I can see him from my table. He is sitting with some other children from the village, watching our monkeys scamper and play.

"A Thai Dam lad was brought here last week also; his name is Tao Koo. Several months ago he had a fever of some kind, and severe diarrhea with stomach cramps. His parents put him to the mat, and I suppose the village witch-doctor incanted something or other. As is the usual case amongst primitive people, he was kept out of the sunlight (evil) and fresh air (poisonous to a sick person). He was given only rice and water, which are inadequate any time and horribly so to a sickened one. Within two weeks the child developed a bed sore on his sacrum, and within a month it had spread until all the flesh from his buttocks was destroyed. Over each hip two ulcers appeared. He became incontinent, and this constant soilage only worsened things. He came to us ravaged, full of contamination and corruption. Wet rot, rankled flesh, decaying bones, polluted beyond belief. His mentality suffered too, he became apathetic, stolid and indifferent. Ever see a little kid who wouldn't laugh or even cry?

"Earl and Dwight immediately took Tao Koo to their hearts, and lucky is that boy. They took the wisp of a body that was left, and with all the tenderness they could muster they bathed him, debrided the dirty globs of flesh, and thoroughly cleaned him up. With the hearts of men and the hands of women, they gently but firmly bandaged him in cool, clean dressings. The boy showed no reaction. He was too deadened by pain to respond to even this much compassion.

"The boys rigged a special bed for him. Balloons were tied across the top bars, and pictures stapled to the wall low to the bed so the boy could see them while lying on his belly. They gave him a color book and a rabbit that squeaked. "During the sunlight hours—right now—they bring his bed outside. A mosquito net is draped over to keep the flies off the sores. All dressings are removed and mother-sun helps to dry up his still-raw sores.

"But already Tao Koo, eyes last week so bleak with dying, is beginning to brighten. His terrified family have learned to bathe him daily and feed him properly. Vitamins, minerals, proteins nourish him along with his rice and water. Dwight and Earl even rigged a contraption to prevent the child's incontinency from soiling everything.

"Teresa, this wistful little lad is a soul. He is God's compromise between flower and dung . . . God's interval between birth and death. And he is important as *one*. In this age of antibiotics, increasing specialization, and fancy electronic laboratory methods, we doctors sometimes lose sight of our primary function, 'the care of patients.' These two boys, Earl and Dwight, in the earliest stage of their medical training, have not lost sight, nor will they. Their task in life is burned into their hearts . . . to cure sometimes . . . to relieve often . . . to comfort always. What fine doctors they'll be! The emaciated little Tao Koo, now filling out, healing up, is a great credit to my team. And he is one of dozens and dozens who come to us daily.

The Joy of Our Work

"Just now I look out the opened door. The hospital is behind me to the right, the boys are sitting around Tao Koo's bed, the monkeys are playing on their chain nearby, and Guntar is being rocked on Dwight's leg. The range of mountains around us are purple, and I have an immense and quiet happiness here. There is terrible danger, certainly. We were horribly maligned and attacked on Radio Peking last week. Often there is a feeling of terrible hopelessness here, of so much we *cannot* do. But watching these two young men keeps reminding me that even though we may be daily plunged in sickness and misery, there is something good dominant. Watching these two young men now reassures me that the human spirit can rise supreme. As long as men possess the gift of life, they *can* develop the feeling of oneness with other men. And all beings of blood and breath are brothers, Teresa. It is so evident here. We are here to help each other . . . This is our highest calling. The channels are many . . . and mine is the easiest because I am so plunged into the stinking reality of it all. For those in more protected areas, for New Yorkers, it may be harder, because the channels are deep and sometimes hard to navigate. But they are there. In helping us the way you are doing, you illustrate that you've found your way to serve . . . Now we can be instruments of His mercy.

"But I'm muttering a lot and going on and on. Don't want to write so much that you cannot read it all. Keep up the good work for us on accounta we certainly need you. And we love you all too . . . muchly. I mean it, TOM."

The day on which I read this letter was a foggy, rainy day in Manhattan. My father's illness had reached the critical stage, and in two days we were to gather round his bed at Mary Immaculate Hospital reciting rosary after rosary. He died with all of us around him, and it was particularly comforting to me to see two beautiful Dominican nuns hovering over him, and Lou O'Connor ministering to his physical needs. It ended a long, painful siege of illness. I was mindful of those people elsewhere in the world who could not get a doctor, or who did not have access to the pain-killing drugs that were ours if we needed them. It was a terribly sad time and a period in which one needed God desperately every minute of the day. Daily Mass and prayers helped, good friends made the burden lighter, and my involvement and interest in Dr. Dooley's work helped too.

How wise God is that He shields the future from us. A dear friend of mine in a convent had said to me, when my father reached the critical stage of his illness, that I should make a complete act of resignation. I found that this helped a lot. Then Tom wrote, "Tess, I know losing your father was a blow, but it was better when he was suffering so, that he go to a more peaceful place. How good it is to be so sure he died in the best of circumstances soulwise. Would that we could all be so sure! Know you'll keep the chin up and keep plugging away." It turned out that keeping my chin up proved to be a full-time challenge in the days ahead. But Tom's sympathy was very welcome, and what he said was true. After so much pain, I was mindful of the thought that "death is not extinguishing the candle, it is just putting out the light before the dawn."

Chapter VI

THE ROOT OF THE TREE

Tom's work and its progress, especially as he described it in his frequent and vivid letters were real inspirations to me. I realized I might have often found myself immobilized in front of a television set, or wasted my time otherwise, had it not been for the verbal sharing of his work and his problems that Dr. Dooley offered us. At times I wished I didn't have to work for a living so that I could devote full time to helping him.

Lou O'Connor visited Mrs. Dooley in St. Louis around the end of February, and was shown "the museum," as Tom's mother called it. Tom's awards, pictures, diplomas, certificates, honorary degrees, and citations were beautifully framed and hung throughout the apartment, including the long entrance foyer. Mrs. Dooley was particularly fond of a picture that Bishop Fulton J. Sheen had inscribed for her, citing the tremendous need in Asia and pointing out that her son was truly a missionary.

As we got more involved with Tom's work, it became a common occurrence to get a phone call from a total stranger. One day a Mr. Weintraub called me to give us Tom's love and, as he said, to "needle" us about our reluctance to make the trip to Laos. I gathered that Mr. Weintraub was Laos-bound himself, and for a moment I thought he was going to ask us to fly with him. We finished our pleasant conversation, and with mixed emotions I hung up the phone and went back to work. We found out later that Mr. Weintraub was the president of an advertising concern that handled the account for the Willys jeeps. We also learned that he wasn't going to Laos himself, but was arranging for a camera crew in Bangkok to do a photographic story at Muong Sing. Yet Tom kept urging us to come, predicting that we would "hitch a ride yet." He had been on a 15-day river trip and had spent a week in Vientiane; he and the boys finished the new building in a rush so the Crown Prince could see it. Tom also made some KMOX broadcasts, wrote two articles and dozens of business letters but, he said, there were about 300 letters still facing him. It got to the point where I tried to be succinct in my letters and itemized important things for his attention, to save his precious little time.

Many moments were spent in trying to figure out ways to bolster the morale of the team in Muong Sing. One day we decided to make a tape for Tom, Dwight, Earl and the others. After we arranged a few glasses (beside the mike), and with a metal letter opener we kept clinking them so that it sounded like the background you'd hear in Connelly's "Sweet Shoppe," as Tom called the restaurant. When the tape reached Laos, Tom reported, the boys "roared, loved the accents, the thoughts, and the constant tinkling in the background." This was one time I think we had more fun then he did. It happened to be a day when there was static in the air, and every time Madeline O'Brien's turn came to say a few words, and she touched the tape recorder, she got a shock and would break up laughing, forgetting what she wanted to say. This accounted for much of the hilarity Tom found in the tape and the mistaken impression that we were all "under the influence."

A letter Tom wrote April 20 caused more merriment. "Tragedy, gloom, doom" he started out. "TERESA turned on her back and slid into a buffalo wallow. Came out stinking, but nothing broken. The Filipinos in Vientiane were driving the jeep on a village road with four in back and three in the cabin. TERESA, in a very lady-like manner, simply slid off the roadside and gently, ever so gently, turned turtle. The buffalo wallow had mud six feet deep, so no one was hurt. They said that all you could see sticking out of the mud was the underchassis. They wrote and said they were all suing me, as *certainly* TERESA MLI had insurance. With the help of half a dozen water buffalo and the Filipinos, the jeep was dragged out on her back, righted, and later hauled away. Within a week she was running again, perky and prim, but a slight mist of buffalo cologne all over her."

This letter also contained the seed for his unborn book, *The Night They Burned the Mountain*. Tom wrote, "Kathleen writes that flowers are pushing out of the crusty old earth back there in America. Here everything is falling back into the earth. Trees fall, the jungle decomposes, paint rolls off the walls, and thatch blows off the roof. These are early monsoons, the season when the frog eats the moon. The wind blows a lot, and the villagers fear this season so. They believe evil spirits are everywhere. At night the villagers throw firecrackers into the sky to scare the evil spirits away. Most eerie is the night when they burn the mountain. The Kha Kho tribesman burn the mountain-jungle slopes, and plant their rice into the blackened-scorched earth.

"Little Guntar was discharged the other day, walking. He is fine, and we were able to jump the obstacle of anguish, the language barrier. Compassion speaks in unconscious ways, I guess. Earl's pet patient (and project), Tao Koo, goes home in a few days. Although he will never walk again, he is in good health, has strong tissues, and a good frame of mind. In his bright little mind he can walk the sky.

"The enclosure, if you haven't figured it out by now, is a bat wing. The bats here tumble and dart. This one Si caught just for you (with a cake cover). How would you like some insects, so huge they hush and cluck and flutter about? Little momentoes like this make you feel 'near' to us don't they?

"The ABC team is in Vientiane; and I imagine they will be coming up in a few days. Two weeks of them. Hope we can face it. Sometimes photographers are great, aiming at spontaneity, but the ones who say, 'Hold that, doctor,' 'Turn the baby over again,' 'Oops, face the light a bit more'—hate that type.

"Much, much to do yet, though at last we are caught up on surgery. The Minister of Social Welfare sent 100 sheets of corrugated sheet metal so we have put ceilings in the clinic's three rooms. This is really much cleaner and safer than the woven bamboo mats that we had nailed to cross wooden bars. And it helps to fulfill my idea of having the Lao build this hospital themselves. Much love to all, especially Tess during tough times."

Offers of help started to appear as a result of the article

The Root of the Tree

Tom had encouraged me to write for *The Tablet,* and this made us feel good. We received mail from high school and college teachers who said that we were the recipients of their blessings and prayers, and their hopes that Tom's work would flourish. This inspired us even further.

Mrs. Dooley confided in us that there was a possibility of Tom appearing on the *This Is Your Life* television program. This really was a *big* secret that we were entrusted with, and we never divulged the fact that we had known there was such a possibility. We still had not met Mrs. Dooley, but her letters were warm and sincere. She was particularly grateful for our *Dr. Dooley News Bulletins,* and as she put it herself she felt "so close and akin" to us.

Overseas, in the meantime, an eerie silence settled on the hospital compound in Muong Sing. The ABC people had finished their job, and their departure in a chartered Beaver left the village and the hospital in a quiet state of normalcy. To liven things up a bit, Tom thought up a wild idea. At meal time he felt he could have a lot of fun if each man had his own special coffee mug. Walter Connell, whose hobby was ceramics, agreed to make the mugs according to Tom's hand-sketched specifications. And what specifications they were! One mug was to have the shape of an elephant; another, that of a torso; Ngoan's mug was to be a big foot with a bandaid on the toe; another, a molar tooth with a bloody root for one of the boys who wanted to be a dentist. Finally, there was a big green mug for Tom, and as an added attraction, without Tom knowing anything about it, Walter put a little ceramic frog in the bottom of the mug. When they were ready we packed them with great care using sponges, bandages, mopheads to cushion them as we were well aware that this box, like others, could be dropped by parachute from a plane. Each item we used to cushion the mugs could be used in the hospital; in this way we wasted no money in packing a box. We had to sit back and wait to see if they arrived in one piece.

Tom wrote that his idea of a luxurious break from Muong Sing was to "wallow in a hot tub at the Hotel Erawan in Bangkok, and slop up chocolate ice cream." But if he tarried too long there, he would miss the "cool mountain valley and chaos of the sick-call line."

His letter of May 6th told us he would definitely come home in November, as the Criss Award dinner was scheduled to be held around November 10th. Tom had a backlog of some 400 letters and I suggested that he use a mimeographed reply letter, but he would have no part of that idea. He felt that if people took the trouble to write him, the least he could do was answer them. While in a beautiful city like Bangkok, where most people were sightseeing and shopping, Tom Dooley was hunting for a public stenographer to answer the people whose letters meant so much to him. One letter from a member of a religious order said: "It isn't often we find one who really fulfills his ideals. When someone performs noble and even heroic deeds, we realize that there are still many good people left in this world."

Tom's letter of May 11th said he wasn't willing to accept a "no" to our going to Muong Sing, but promised we would talk about it when he was home in November. He advised us to take our regular vacation, and "we'll talk about the future in a few months." Kay and I went ahead and completed our plans for a trip to the Caribbean in

October, figuring we would need all the rest we could get before Tom's arrival in New York in November.

We had kept a record of the number of people who had seen Tom's home-made film of his work and the score at this time was 2,000. When we were asked to send the film to Villanova University for a showing to 500 sisters, we were delighted. This was surely on audience with a great potential wattage, sometimes referred to as "candlelight," in the Christophers' sense. One sister wrote, "Just to know that there is such a noble soul responding to God's call makes your heart thrill and love God more."

Our efforts on behalf of Tom's work now received formal recognition in a personal acknowledgment from Mr. Angier Biddle Duke, and the Dr. Dooley Aid Club was officially thanked for its efforts and financial support. Tom reminded us that we had raised nearly a thousand dollars in less than a year, for which he was very grateful. He seemed even more pleased with our adopting the 21 children in Savath's school, all of whose gifts had arrived safely. Tom waited for a slack afternoon to make the two-hour hike in the mud to take pictures of the kids opening the boxes. On the 8th of June, Tom hiked in ankle-deep mud to Savath's school, and arrived to find the school closed. After drinking some "lousy tea" from his canteen, he started the long walk back. The usual shower, dinner and coffee did nothing to make Tom feel more relaxed; he said that the mud sucking at his boots had completely exhausted him.

Around Decoration Day we heard more about TERESA's whereabouts. Tom wrote that "a plane came in today, the first one in several weeks. The landing strip is mostly mud. The 'revolution' in the South has caused all civilian planes in the Kingdom (about 15) to be diverted for troop transportation, and the monsoon rains here just keep crashing down so hard that the sun doesn't dare come out. Compound all this together and you understand a little of the cause of our isolation blended with depression.

"Thought of all of you last night as we were chasing a big bug. He got under a crate that with a small mattress on it serves as a *'chaise longue.'* Around the walls of the house we have these crates that Tess helped me pack so long ago. Well, we decided to open said crate and clean it out, and found lots of things, including some stenciled shirts that we missed." (We had stencilled our MEDICO on each tee-shirt.)

Madeline O'Brien and her friends of the Dooley Aid Club picked up the tab for a Vespa, and Tom wrote: "Delighted you are paying for it, and feel kinda guilty being a two-'car' man. Let me explain the scooter: in Vientiane I used to borrow TERESA when I was down there on business, but TERESA is now up country near my old station of Vang Vieng.

"The monsoon humidity is an unbelievable thing. No laundry dries, the bedding rolls are always clammy, things mildew faster than you can get to them. Surgical instruments have to be kept in oil, our envelopes seal shut, this piece of paper is nearly limp, sweat doesn't evaporate, the mud is so high it sucks at our feet, the compound is a swamp, Earl's cigarettes are 'crummy,' to quote him. . . . etc., etc., etc. There has been no sun for 17 days (we timed it).

"This morning the wind was wailing through the valley like a lament. I went outside for a moment, and as the dawn was burning through just a little I noticed all the palm trees across the field bowing low to the mountain. Thought how much it looked like acolytes bowing at the *Confiteor.*

"I don't know what time I'll be back in November. Peter (Dr. Comanduras) will set it to coincide with the Criss Award Committee. The Tibetan fury has not quieted one iota. Asian papers which arrived today are full of anger and phlegm.

"A Yao boy, whose avulsed scalp (from a fall) we re-attached, is doing fine. Scared to death when we put on the surgical masks, but he didn't seem to be afraid of anything else but that. So we operated under local, *without* masks."

His letters were filled with praise for Dwight and Earl. Tom found they worked long and hard, and had this simple guide—"the best way to achieve one's own happiness is to strive for the happiness of others." Two new expressions were added to the vocabularies of the youngsters in Muong Sing, "O.K. bud," and "Come on."

Tom found much loneliness, danger, choking futility, and a terrible amount of exertion in the work he was doing. He recalled that his teachers told him "humanity is God on earth." And he often spoke of the dream of Anne Frank: "Things will change, and men become good again and these pitiless days will come to an end and the world will once more know order, rest, and peace."

Suddenly Tom was told that he might have to get home sooner than he expected, sometime in October, instead of November. "Although I have no right to be demanding," he wrote, "I hope you and Kathleen won't be in the middle of the West Indies at that time." He ordered a few thousand applicators, some analgesic antiseptic ear-drops and some giant plastic cloths. And more tee-shirts for Dr. Manny Voulgaropoulos.

We were kept busy laying the groundwork for Tom's return in October, planning a reception in his honor at the Hotel Governor Clinton. Though we could not guarantee that Tom would be there, the results of ticket-selling were gratifying, and I wrote Tom and told him about our plans.

After his visit with Dr. Manny in Cambodia, Tom reached Muong Sing on the 4th of July, "home at last." He said he found Kratie dusty and hot. Though Muong Sing had a murky gray heat, it "didn't choke you." Tom advised us to write to Dr. Manny and ask him for projects that the Dooley Aid Club could carry out. He admitted that he needed the "constant bucking up from correspondence that I get." He added: "The hinges that our happiness swings on are really such simple ones." It seemed to me that when things are simple, the human heart asks no questions. To me simplicity, like cleaniness, is next to Godliness. This reminded me that Tom's humor was superbly simple. Simple things could delight him. His happiness was infectious, as was his humor.

When I told Tom that we were "talking big" about his program, he replied: "I think you not only talk big, but *do* pretty damn big too. Do you know the value of what you have sent us in commodities, and the cash you have accrued, and the publicity you earned for us, to say nothing of the personal boost? *Li, li, li.*" (This was Lao for "much, much, much.")

I noticed that in all my hours with Tom he never failed to say thank you. He was constantly pulling little notes or business cards with notes on the back of them out of his pockets and thanking someone for something. But he was always happiest when he was giving.

The next letter from Tom was headed "Out beyond—July 12, 1959, Village of Muong Sing." It was signed "Tom" in red crayon. It was now definite that he would be home the last week of October, "certainly NOT before." He said that the USIS sent him several hundred new paper flags, and Si gave them to some Lao children who pasted them up in their homes. Radio Peking got wind of it and announced that it was "an insidious and imperialistic effort on the part of Dooley to turn the minds of children."

Tom found it wonderful to watch the youthful vigor of his Lao students. They were all flattered that the Thanh Mo America (Dr. America) thought so highly of their ability that he gave them responsibilities while his two American assistants visited Hong Kong, and of course they bent over backwards to do a good job. "One night during this period a tiger-mauling case (man was attacked dawn of that day, and it took 12 hours to stretcher him to the hospital) arrived. There was a lot of patching to be done. We started the generator. The noise can be heard all through this part of the village. Within five minutes all fifteen students were crammed into the little operating room, trying to assist and as a consequence, things were more hectic than they should have been. But they were just trying hard, that's all."

Tom also reported this story. "One of our military outstations had given to the chief of each village in his area some Spectrocin cream (an antibiotic skin cream that we have a great deal of, thanks to Squibb). This lad, one of our students, had instructed the village 'father' in using it, and warned him of the foolishness of using tobacco juice, etc., for wounds. Hence, when the man was mauled, the Pho Ban (Father of the Village) gave the man first-aid himself, neatly spreading this cream over the hideous scalp wound (almost avulsed, all the forehead flopped down over the nose and lip). No one was allowed to put in any of the local concoctions such as cow-dung, bat wings, betel juice, leaves or other witch-doctor hand-me-downs. As a consequence, upon his arrival we had a surgically clean case with no overwhelming infection to deal with first. Things like this are a stimulant to me. These people can and will learn, and can and will apply what they learn. They *do* want change, they are not content with the status quo, they are seeking betterment."

Tom closed by saying that his spirits were high, although the weather was murky. "Go live it up in the West Indies," he advised us, "on accounta you'll need plenty of energy for our meetings and walks. Am really looking forward to pounding those mossless pavements of New York again. Where should we start? See you all in 110 days (more or less)."

It turned out to be less. That October date was destined to be moved up to an August date, and the starting-place he wondered about was to be New York's Memorial Hospital. We still had no inkling that Tom had become gravely ill, and the news was to come suddenly and as a great shock. Yet in these letters written just before his return he kept sounding a note that was sad and gloomy. I thought it had to do with the sad state of political affairs in Laos, and of course in great part it did. The unrest of that summer was a serious matter, Tom told us, and it was creating havoc in the whole area. The villagers lived in dread because of the rumor that a communist battalion was marching down the valley trail from the China frontier. Whenever an alarm sounded, the people waited tense and frightened until the small hours of the morning, when an all-clear was sounded by banging a heavy spoon against a piece of metal.

His last two letters of this period are to my mind remarkable documents. "I know the news here has been grisly," Tom wrote at 3 A.M. on August 10th. "How *well* I know. An American plane landed yesterday (the first one for weeks) with Dwight and Earl rushing back here, and a representative of the Ambassador aboard. The latter brought a letter suggesting—with all the power of the Ambassador's office—that I evacuate my hospital immediately.

"I have refused. The reasons are myriad and manifold, but they can be boiled down to three—my commitment to my publisher, my mason's hands, and to Dooley's inner self. 'The book of me, the root of the tree, the foundation of the building, the heart of it all: I am a doctor.'

"Based on this my duty is clear and precise, just as that of the fireflies in the black night outside my door right now. It is preposterous to think of abandoning the sick and wounded there when they need us most. Perhaps in our small 'candle way' we can show these people, and all Laos, that Americans believe in sticking by their friends in time of need . . . as America's policy is to help free nations when they are threatened and intimidated.

"Laos is moving deeper and deeper in the shadows. I know you understand the geography here. All the fighting is on the Lao–North Viet Nam frontier, and not on ours (China-Burma-Lao). However, there is a large placement of Chinese communist troops on our frontier, so close that

we can practically hear them building their gun enplace-
ments. It would seem that if the fighting along the NVN
frontier does not yield the results that the global plan of
the communist party desires, they might order in the
Chinese troops onto Muong Sing's back and belly.

"So just as the lurid moon tonight spreads over this
primeval land and transfixes it in mountain beauty, atroc-
ity and fear have transfixed Laos, and its fragile peace is
more fragile than ever.

"A plane is due in tomorrow to take the Americans
back, and this note to you, a broadcast to KMOX, etc. I am
told Vientiane is full of war correspondents, so you are
probably more up-to-date on daily developments than we
on the front lines are.

"The little glint of sunlight that I saw only last week is
snuffed out. The thought that in a few days the Lao
government might order me out (and then I *would* go) is
appalling. If Muong Sing falls, my house, my hospital, all
the hundreds and hundreds of hours and small heartfelt
things fall too. If I cannot get all my crew out, they will be
butchered. Twenty heads were impaled on stakes at a
landing strip at Sam Neua province; the pilot came down
to land, saw the heads, understood the grisly warning, and
came over to Muong Sing. I've a special seat at this savage
sideshow. It seems I so often have. I've seen lands and
people's flesh burst forth in scarlet and black wounds.

"The not knowing is the hardest thing. The expecta-
tion. In the trees the monkeys, howling with voices of the
damned, seem frightening. The silence of the valley right
now seems like a whiff of the tomb. Only once before have
I prayed so hard as I am praying now. But all is well, Earl
and Dwight are back with me, we are prepared for what-

ever may come . . . and I'll get another note out as soon as I can."

Five days later: "This is going to be a very quick note. Remember this next line: *'I've a heavy load on my mind just now, and in a small way it is anguish. How glad I will be when I know.'* I'll explain later." We thought the ominous note had to do with the evacuation of Muong Sing. Our concern for his personal safety grew stronger. I resolved to get to Mass more often during the week.

In New York it was a hot Friday in August, with temperatures high in the 90's. At work, I received word that an ABC documentary, entitled *The Splendid American,* narrated by John Daly, was to be shown on television September 27th. I hung up the phone and anxiously tried to make up for lost time on my job. Suddenly the phone rang again.

It was Tom. He was calling from a press conference he was holding in New York! He asked me if I could get the girls together and have an emergency meeting in Connelly's at five. He asked me not to tell the girls he was in the city; it was to be a surprise. After Tom hung up, I had a call from Gloria Sassano, of Medico. She asked me if Tom had told me why he was home. When I said no, she informed me, "He has cancer." I hung up the phone, deeply shocked.

I rounded up but didn't tell the girls, and we sat drinking coffee. I had alerted Gil Murtagh of Tom's imminent arrival, and he had on hand his favorite eclairs and lots of slices of lemon. The girls were delighted when Tom and his brother Malcolm arrived. When the eclairs were served, Tom didn't ask any questions, he just devoured them. Then in a very simple way, he told us why he was home.

He explained that his cancer was a new weapon. He said the only difference between us and him was that he knew how long he had to live, and we did not. He did not want any maudlin press about his illness. While Tom talked, Malcolm thumbed through the late afternoon papers to see how the press conference was reported. Tom went on to say that he had to work faster and harder to get his work done, and he needed our help now more than ever. He asked us to be kind to his mother when she came to the city. He said he would live his life as a Catholic should—a day at a time. There were three choices he could make: become maudlin over his illness, live it up, or do what had to be done. It was obvious which one he chose. He mentioned that he hoped to visit Lourdes.

When Tom and Mal left, we were a sorry lot. Strangers came over to the table to console us. We had a weepy weekend and our hearts and spirits were heavy at this incredible blow. What was it that Tom had written? "The root of the tree . . . the heart of it all: I am a doctor."

Chapter VII

SOMETHING GOOD IN RETURN

A biopsy was performed on Tom upon his arrival at Memorial Hospital and some of the surgeons, in consultation, were reluctant to perform an operation. They felt that Tom had only a short time to live and that the operation and its attendant pain would prolong his life merely a few more months. Tom insisted on the surgery.

On Monday, August 24, we went up to Memorial Hospital armed with good intentions and vows to laugh, smile, and make the visit just as pleasant as possible. We were shocked to find the hospital corridor full of television cameras, technicians, producers, and whatnot. With Tom's permission, CBS was to do a film on the entire operation. It had a dual purpose, to help give courage to other people with cancer and to help Tom's work. They planned to show Tom being prepared for the operation, the actual surgery, his convalescence, and even his return trip. All of us had mixed emotions about the whole idea. We found Tom in bed, with freshly applied television makeup, but he still looked so thin and so sick.

The mail poured in to Memorial Hospital, much of it containing donations. Tom would read it and grin and say, "With every cross I get from God, I get something good in return." Tom was sure that, because of his illness, God would be generous in other ways. In answer to some letters, Tom said that it did not matter how long a man lived, but rather what he did with every minute. He said he was not about to give up. God had given him a terrible cancer, "and He wants me to use it."

Many good friends were to write to us during these trying days. One in particular that I have never forgotten went as follows: "Dr. Dooley is marked out by God . . . to do great work for God and man. The impact Dr. Dooley has made on people is not his doing, it is God's. And his impact will go on years and years . . . To read his letters and to read his books brings God so near and makes one long to serve God better. Men have said that just hearing about him makes them want to be better men. Doctor Tom is just God's instrument—a keen, highly gifted, sensitive, noble soul, fashioned by God for this work and magnificently surrendered to the holy will of God. *Of such stuff saints are made.*"

Tom always disliked hearing himself called a saint, and during his life I could agree with him that it was embarrassing. Of course he was a very human person. But then, how does one judge a saint? By his whole life and motivation? By his compassion and sacrifices, or by his human frailties? The future will have to judge Dr. Dooley, but it is worth remembering that the Church defines as saints everyone who is reunited with God after death, not merely those people who are proclaimed saints here below.

While Tom was undergoing the three-hour televised

operation on Thursday, August 27th, I met Mrs. Dooley at the airport. It was our first meeting, and the more I came to know this woman who had so much tragedy in her life, the more I admired her.

It was many months later that Tom had the courage to watch the CBS films of the operation. It was certainly a strange state of affairs to see yourself being operated on. One of my chief recollections of the film was the constant clunking sound made by the hemostats as the doctor deftly cut away the dead cancerous tissue. I realize now that Tom's insistence on the surgery actually gained him almost a year and a half during which he was to do some of his greatest work.

Several days after the operation, an elderly friend dropped by to visit Tom. As he made his way down the corridor, aided by his cane, the redoubtable gentleman was startled to see his young friend Tom being whisked by in a stretcher, draped in surgical garments. When Tom shouted to him, "I'll be right back," the old man was even more bemused, but he continued on to Tom's room to wait for him. A few minutes later the door to Tom's room opened. True to his word, there was Tom Dooley, hopping off the stretcher. He explained that he had had to do a retake for the TV cameras, and the old man mopped his brow in relief.

During the time of Tom's hospitalization, a world-wide prayer crusade was begun by a young lady at the headquarters of the *Catholic Digest*. We were called in to help with her amazing undertaking during the final hours of the huge job. She had sent a request for special prayers to the Little Flower, St. Thérèse of Lisieux, to all the Carmelite nuns and priests, Trappist monks and nuns, Poor

Clare nuns, and Jesuit Fathers, to name a few of the religious orders. The 12-day crusade was to end on Tuesday, September 8th, the Feast of the Nativity of our Blessed Mother.

We were only too glad to be able to do something constructive during these terrible days, and it was a real privilege to have a part in the stuffing, stamping, and final midnight mailing of these letters. As we dumped the last shopping bag at the 34th Street Post Office, I found myself smiling and saying, "NOW we'll see what happens." I must say I had a feeling of peace. How could God let down someone who had been so good to the least of His? What would be His answer to all these prayers? We could only wait and see. A daily Mass at the altar of the Little Flower was being said at 8 A.M. in St. Patrick's Cathedral, and I made it a point to be on hand each day.

In one of my visits to the hospital, I told Tom about the crusade, and he was deeply touched. After receiving the special novena prayer, a New York woman made hundreds of copies of it and distributed them to her office associates. Twenty newly ordained Maryknoll Fathers, en route to the African missions, promised before their departure to offer their Masses and Holy Communions aboard ship for Tom's cure. A young woman in Manhattan personally distributed 100 copies of the prayer and then translated it into German for her family in Bavaria; her family wrote and told her that they had pledged almost all of their totally Catholic village to the prayer crusade.

The surgeons had amazing news. Extensive x-ray examinations of the lungs and bones showed no evidence of metastasis, or spreading of the tumor. In addition, Tom's convalescence had been termed "excellent." Within two days he had regained his normal appetite and was walking around. Tom had skin grafted from his knees to his chest. And both areas were raw and sore.

Tom was discharged from the hospital on the first Sunday of the month, the day before Labor Day. Gloria Sassano and I were there to lend a hand. It wasn't long before my Hudson was loaded to the roof with Tom's lightweight aluminum luggage, his ever-present tan case with the safe lock, his typewriter, gifts, flowers, and bags of mail. Most prized of all the gifts Tom received were sculptured busts of Lincoln and Dr. Schweitzer, done by Leo Cherne. Tom was very thin, his arm was in a black sling, but his spirits were high. I do not recall that he ever once complained about pain. We drove to the Waldorf and helped him up to his room. Tom's arrival was hailed by a fellow native of St. Louis, a lovely and beautiful woman named Ann Walsh Weiler, who handled publicity for the Waldorf and who now serves on our Board of Trustees.

Tom unpacked his few personal belongings. Normally his luggage contained pocketbooks made of Lao cloth, weighty native jewelry, swords, bowls, opium weights that his patients gave him, and anything else that caught his fancy as a gift for someone. But this day, as he looked about him, he saw that he was inundated with mail. While in the past he tackled a great deal of it personally, he realized that now, with his arm in a sling, he had a problem.

The prayer crusade ended on Labor Day, and there weren't many people in St. Patrick's or even in the city on that holiday. Carol Cantwell, though, was there. I didn't know her then, but she was to become very much a part of our work. As she left the church, Dr. Dooley tore up the steps, hoping to get there in time for *his* Mass. Because he could not get his jacket on over the sling, he wore a long-sleeved white shirt. Carol stood staring after him, in a mild state of shock. The last she had heard, Dr. Dooley was still in Memorial Hospital. She had come to pray for him all during the novena, and now here he was himself, on the last day of the prayer crusade! This chance encounter began her long and dedicated devotion and she has diligently shared her time between the New York Foundling Hospital and Tom's work.

After Mass several of us walked back to the Waldorf and had breakfast with Tom. We were so pleased to see him eat well. He told us of his concern for the safety of Dwight and Earl, still holding the fort in Laos. The news reports, telling daily of the encroachment of red troops throughout the country, were no consolation to a man who was trying to recuperate.

The next day I set about trying to find a solution to the problem of Tom's mail. My idea had to do with some kind of dictating machine—something that would not be too heavy for him to carry, since he was planning to keep his lecture dates. I called a fellow named Tom Earles, who worked in the Coordination Division of my company, and explained Dr. Dooley's need. Tom Earles was a Notre Dame graduate, so I felt he would at least hear me out. He said he thought he knew of a little machine that would help, and he brought it around to show it to me. What he found was a SoundScriber. It weighed about six pounds, and my brain tried to memorize every last feature of it so I could explain it to Tom.

Unknown to me, Tom had been thinking of another solution to his problem. A day or so later, Mr. McGurk's telephone rang at the office and, as he spoke, I thought I heard my name mentioned. I became even more curious when it was mentioned in connection with the Personnel Officer of the company. Tom had gone to the top, to the President of the Metropolitan Life Insurance Company, to ask for help. All he wanted was my services for a period of six months! Actually, as he told me later, he was aiming for three months but played it safe by asking for six. While I don't know all that was said over the phone that day, there was talk of insurance, vacations, and a temporary replacement for me.

The next day Tom came in person to see Mr. McGurk. He wasn't taking any chances. Mr. Joseph J. Carney, my present boss, was in the office with Mr. McGurk at the time. When I looked into Mr. McGurk's office, to see what had occasioned the sudden commotion, there was Tom on one knee, making his appeal. Before Tom left, Joe Carney said, "Jim, why don't you give him your furniture as well?" When the good-natured bantering was finished, the deal was clinched with Tom's gift to Mr. McGurk, a little brass monkey which had its hands over its eyes. Tom said, "This will serve to remind you for a while, Mr. McGurk, to see no evil, hear no evil, and speak no evil." The monkey remained in the same spot on Mr. McGurk's desk until I packed it away with his personal belongings when he retired in 1964.

I learned that I would be permitted a three-month leave of absence, beginning immediately, to work with Dr. Dooley. Fortunately Tom had no objections to the vacation that Kay and I had planned so long ago "so that we could be rested when Tom got home from Laos." I told Tom I was sure he could get someone better qualified than

I to help him. When he replied that he had asked for *me*, I wondered silently how I would ever be able to keep up with him on a full-time basis.

Tom started getting phone calls from people who wanted to help him. Among these callers were New York secretaries, many of whom are still working as volunteers in the Thomas A. Dooley Foundation. Tom referred all these girls to me, and we formed a group called the Disc Girls. They were assigned the job of taking dictation from Tom's SoundScriber discs, and this machine did turn out to be the perfect solution to Tom's correspondence problem. Our office space in the Graybar Building at 420 Lexington Avenue was donated by Mr. William Zeckendorf. My company donated some used furniture that suited Tom's present needs, now that Medico was dissociated from the International Rescue Committee, and had decided to fly on its own wings.

Most new business offices open up and wait for the mail, but in our case the mail was waiting for us before we opened. Tom had begun his lecture tour, and he was hardly over the first few television interviews when the letters started coming in, bundled in huge canvas mailsacks.

To work with Tom, I soon found out you had to be ready to spring into action at a moment's notice. You had to be able to set up an office in an airline terminal, a cab, a limousine, a bus, a hotel lobby, or just any place. It was a far cry from the pace I was accustomed to on 23rd Street. I was always busy there, but at least I knew where I would be working.

The files we had brought with us from IRC were still unpacked, and I ached to see them opened and put into place. I looked about the office and wondered what color the walls should be painted. I wanted Tom to see his office in shape before he left for Laos. Maybe he'd think of it overseas and it would brighten up his days.

The mail came to us from all directions. After the checks, money-orders, and cash donations were recorded and receipted by a very competent girl named Vivian Cristol, some of the mail was turned over to me. I also got it from Tom, together with his discs. Betty Moul and Kay Scanlan, both of whom then worked for U.S. Steel, were the earliest volunteers in this work, and nothing was too much for them. Working late at night and weekends during the winter when the heat was turned off seemed to pose no problems for them. As time went on and the hurdles got steeper, I would think of Tom's words: "The reward for service is the strength to serve."

Finally Kay Kelly and I boarded the *Nieuw Amsterdam* for our cruise. I was so tired that I could hardly make the boat. I had been too busy to shop for new clothes, but I was looking forward to the rest and to being away from a telephone. "Away from it all" was our motto, and we promised ourselves we would tell no one that we worked for the Metropolitan and Dr. Dooley. Then, at the first lifeboat drill aboard ship, a girl in a brightly colored life-preserver approached us and said she was a member of the Dr. Dooley Aid Club of the Metropolitan. Hadn't she seen us before? We should have known that it wouldn't take long for our "secret" to get out.

We were not permitted to forget about the nature of Tom's work, either. When we stopped at Haiti, we saw at first-hand the full realities of sickness and poverty. We saw families piling their meager belongings around telephone poles and calling this "home." Bathed in sunlight and surrounded with Christmas poinsettias, the island's beauty was breathtaking, yet one noticed that there were daily burials of children. Even a walk in the iron market, where little girls kneeled on curbstones and washed their hair in the streets, cast ominous shadows on the purple splendor of Haiti.

We returned home rested and anxious to see Tom. I invariably had mixed emotions about these meetings, and Kay got tired of hearing me express concern about not being able to keep up with Tom's capacity for work, his speedy dictation, and the myriad duties that seemed to crop up faster than I could cope with them. However, once I got back into the swing of things, all fears vanished. Tom constantly expressed satisfaction, and it wasn't long before the question was raised about my working for him on a permanent basis. This was a new thought for me to consider, with many ramifications, but for the time being we put it aside, and I reached out and accepted all the help I could get.

As Tom made his way across the country giving talks about his work, the office began taking on the appearance of a warehouse. Medicines, clothing, soap, and toys now came in with the letters. One day the switchboard operator referred a call to me, and as it turned out, this was one of the best things that ever happened to Tom Dooley. The caller, Paul Hellmuth, was interested in meeting with Tom. An attorney and a trustee of Notre Dame, Paul had been invited to attend a "Splendid American Award" dinner in Boston, honoring Tom, but he had not been able to make it. After reading the account in the newspapers the next day, he decided he must meet this Tom

Dooley and did so the next evening at a benefit in New York. They both had plans to travel to Washington, so they made arrangements to fly down together. It was the beginning of a great friendship.

When Paul came to our office and looked about, he saw the need not only for equipment, but for more space. Sitting in the so-called reception room, surrounded by the pungent odor of vitamin pills and drugs, he confirmed his first impression that somebody had to step in and help. Through his initiative and drive, much was accomplished. First, we secured new quarters on another floor of the Graybar Building, which turned out to be the office that Tom had dreamed about. It was equipped with its own conference room, a real reception room, and several small offices. Through Paul's efforts, a volunteer group agreed to pay the rent and took care of the decorating. Among other things, he got us a duplicating machine and tables for the typewriters. All we had to do was indicate a need, and somehow he found a way to fill it. It will no doubt embarrass Paul to read here that all of us considered him our Prince Charming, and still do. His loyalty and aid can never be measured.

I marveled at the letters we received. In particular, the mail from young Americans impressed me because my own youth had been preoccupied with having a good time, and taking nice vacations. My country, like my God, meant much to me, and I always felt a concern for its welfare. But, although I supported the missions, I was not too concerned with poverty and illness in the world. So it was an eye-opener for me to come upon young people who heard lectures given by Dr. Dooley, or read his books and felt a personal responsibility to people in foreign lands.

Tom always tried to write personal notes to the young people who took an interest in his work.

The hours at 420 Lexington Avenue were long, especially when Tom was in the city. Sometimes he combined work with pleasure. He would be in the middle of dictating a letter and someone would telephone or drop by. The next thing I knew, I was invited out for dinner. Riding in the cab, another idea might strike Tom, and I'd find myself taking shorthand again.

Sometimes I used Tom's room at the hotel as an office when he was out of town. I found I was able to catch up on more work there, as the interruptions were fewer than at Medico headquarters. But when Tom got back, he'd have dozens of new assignments, and out of his pockets would tumble all sorts of notes he had made. Priority notes, on thin folds of paper, were slipped through his ring and stayed there until they had been dealt with.

One night Kay and I worked with Tom very late, and we decided that she would stay overnight with me. We had two shopping bags full of mail to be acknowledged, most of it containing cash donations. When we reached my home on Long Island, I found that I was without my keys. We thought we could get in through a window, but as usual my mother had locked them all. Then we suddenly realized what would happen if a policeman came along and saw us prowling around a darkened house with shopping bags full of money! These thoughts caused us to howl with laughter, awakening my mother. While she made no comment as she let us in, I am sure she wondered how many more predicaments we would become involved in for Tom Dooley.

All through these hectic days, we had what I like to

Original members of the
Dr. Dooley Aid Club, 1957.
Left to right, Kay Kelly,
Teresa Gallagher, Dorothy
McCann and Madeline
O'Brien.

Right: Drs. George and
Mary Papanicolaou with
Kay Kelly and Teresa
Gallagher.

Below: The kelly-green
jeep, "Teresa, M.L.I."

Left: **Dr. Dooley,
Teresa Gallagher and
Martin McKneally.**

Below: Metropolitan Li[
Insurance luncheon, 195

Airport departure for Asia, 1958.

With Dooley supporters at the airport.

Dr. Dooley addressing the Disc Girls.

At the dictating machine with the Disc Girls.

With Archbishop Iakovos, Cardinal Spellman,
Henry Cabot Lodge, and Spyros Skouras.

Above: Three views of the stained-glass window in
St. Camilla's Church, Arlington, Mass.

Opposite: Dictating in his plane seat, 1960.

At the airport on his last trip to Asia.

Dr. Verne Chaney and Mrs. Agnes Dooley beside the mobile clinic at Monterey, Cal. after the incorporation of The Thomas A. Dooley Foundation.

Miss Gallagher and Mrs. Dooley in San Francisco on the same occasion.

think of as a "rear echelon" of prayer. Mother M. Doyle of the Convent of Our Lady of the Cenacle was its total membership. The pace, the volume, the problems were such that we needed to know that somebody was praying along with us. Tom often mentioned "the Mystical Body" (all the members of the Church) in his letters. I always felt that his work was very special and necessary, and for some unknown reason there was never a question in my mind about its importance, although many around me felt that the sickness and poverty in America needed attention first.

While Tom worried about how he could get money to keep his program alive, I was concerned about his health. I prayed that God would give him the strength to do what had to be done.

Our rear echelon of prayer, Mother Doyle, reported that student nurses on retreat asked her if she ever heard of Dr. Dooley. "Ha! I punned, 'I am Dooley impressed.' It was delightful to hear them rave about this wonderful doctor," she wrote, "and what rejoiced my heart was to hear them refer all this to God. God using Dr. Tom Dooley. Then they—nineteen-year oldsters—confided that they were ashamed that they have done nothing to help suffering humanity. How do you like that for God's work through Dr. Tom? More than ever you are in my prayers considering the decision you have to make . . . Never, for the rest of your life," she predicted, "will you have any other driving interest but Tom's work, and no matter where you work you will be a propagandist for that."

Chapter VIII

THE DISC TEAM CARRIES ON

One day Tom and I took a cab out to Midwood High School in Brooklyn. Al Harris, a new recruit for Tom's team in Viet Nam, came along. The students had been working to help Tom, and they wanted to present the check which was the result of their efforts. Al and I took a front seat in the school auditorium. Tom went up to the stage with the principal and members of the class, one of whom was Lois Snitkoff. There were two speeches before Lois' talk, and I knew it was her turn to speak when I saw her wetting her lips and checking her notes. Then as Tom was introduced and stepped to the podium, Lois gave her presentation speech. When she hesitated, Tom thought she was through and reached out and took the check, starting to thank her for it. But Lois was *not* through! To Tom's delight, she grabbed the check back and continued with her speech, undismayed by the amusement of her audience. When she completed her presentation, Tom kissed the determined young lady on the cheek, and this too, was accepted by Lois with aplomb.

In early December the girls in the office presented Tom with a woolen sweater at a luncheon. He was planning his return to Laos; he wanted to be back in time for Christmas in Muong Sing, cancer or no cancer. His arm was still weak, his leg and chest still sore from the skin graft. When he shaved, he had to steady his hand by leaning his elbow against the wall.

We sent out word that Tom wanted gifts for his kids in Laos, and soon there were numerous small packages under the tiny Christmas tree we had set up in his hotel room.

Tom's sights were raised as Medico grew, and he now had high hopes of raising a million dollars. A check from Vice President Nixon for $500 did much to bolster his spirits. Margaret Maloney presented to Tom a cash contribution from her fellow-workers at General Motors. Having heard him plead for "cold cash," Margaret had the money packed in dry ice. Tom was delighted by this gag, and mentioned the gift on the Jack Paar show just before he left for Laos. From that time on, volunteer Margaret Maloney has been known affectionately as Cold Cash Maloney, and is presently an officer of the New York City Chapter.

One of Tom's gifts to the office was an Oriental gong with a clapper. Every time a check for $1,000 was received in the mail, the gong was sounded and a happy cheer went up from the staff.

Before Tom left, he was presented with the Criss Award, appeared on the "This Is Your Life" television program, and as guest of honor at a $100 a plate dinner, was handed a check for $25,000 by Conrad Hilton, who said, "This will give you wings to carry on your errands of mercy." Thus Tom was able to realize his dream of purchasing an airplane.

Another highlight of his trip to the West Coast was his visit to Immaculate Heart College, where he was received by an enthusiastic group of young people. Young Ngoan flew in with him, and Sandra Hannum was there to welcome them. Tom's speech was recorded, and to this day it is still in demand. I am told it is still played in various Retreat Houses around the country.

A departure for Asia was always something out of the ordinary. Tom would be all set, and the next day the whole itinerary had to be changed. Before he could put a foot on the plane, I had all kinds of duties to perform— getting tickets, visas, instructions to his office on bank accounts, his own check book, preparing his meetings in connection with new policies and procedures, thank-you letters, and good-bye letters.

At this time I had to ask my company for an extension of my leave of absence to January 18. Once again, the proposal of working permanently for Tom came up. While I wanted to do it, I wondered if I would accomplish as much if I were to do the work on a permanent basis. Working as a volunteer I felt I was in a better position to attract others as volunteers. It seemed to me that if I gave up something, just as Tom was doing, others would be willing to give up something too. And I firmly believe that people respond to example, particularly if there is a sacrifice involved. I promised Tom that somehow we would get his work done and continue to operate as if I were working full time for him.

A farewell party was held for Tom at Pan American's VIP Lounge at the airport on the night of December 17. The office staff, Paul Hellmuth, members of the Laos Embassy, and many volunteers were there to see him off. A chocolate cake, baked for Tom by one of the volunteers, suddenly appeared on this cosmopolitan scene. A short time later I was amused to see that our guest of honor was enjoying even the crumbs; Tom was holding the cake tin close to his chin as he mingled with his guests.

Tom's departure left me tired, but in addition there seemed to be a huge void in the city. It seemed empty and remained a cold, silent giant until a letter with foreign stamps arrived. Then New York became warm, vibrant, and alive again, and I dug in harder. Tom wrote that he couldn't find his 401A's. I wondered what had happened to them, for I distinctly remembered packing camera film inside his shirt collars to help keep them stiff. It wasn't until after I had thrown a camera shop into a frenzy looking for "401A film" that I got word that what Tom wanted was a type of intravenous injection.

Another handwritten letter with the date-line Bangkok, said, "Dear Teresa: In all the maddening flurry and scurry of my 'last days' I do not believe I ever adequately (does one ever?) thanked you for the thousands of hours of work you gave to me. Words often ring hollow exactly when you wish them to be most mellow. In all sincerity, and with deep affection, Teresa, *'cup chai li'* (thanks very much). All the hundreds of thousands of wretched, who this year will be a little less wretched, roll their thanks to you too.

"I hope some of the chaos has simmered down, though a little turmoil is a good thing. Would love to know how much we finally made . . . excluding the money from the movie rights (which probably isn't in yet). And isn't today Mrs. Carroll Day, when she promised to send the $50,000? I'm in Bangkok waiting for the plane. Situation is bad because the Vientiane Embassy was closed Thursday through Sunday. Hence if pilot did send a cable there telling me of the delay, no one was there to forward it to me here.

"Now that I've been sleeping without my manuscript, I have lots of new ideas for it. I am anxiously awaiting the polished manuscript (not galleys, as they are rather unchangeable). I have notes here so I can return the manuscript Bob Giroux sends me as quickly as possible. Time out for cramps. Don't feel so hot, but it is probably to be expected. A mixture of psychological slump and tropical steamy heat. I dread being slowed down. What time there is left is so precious.

"Why didn't I scout out a replacement for me? He can work with me and alternately run Houei Sai. He must be of such a bizarre personality to be my Number 2 that I certainly should have looked for him personally. He should be very young, preferably a bachelor (though not essential), and aggressive enough to be capable but devoted to TAD enuff to be content always to be Number 2, at least as long as I'm in Laos. If we could find an M.D. like Copenhaver it would be perfect. Give it some thought and glance over the M.D. applications. He need volunteer for only one year. But we need him here before I come home in May . . . Cramps again. I just meant this to be a thank you letter, but as usual the verbiage flows. Give some restricted love to my other 'graces,' and to you an everlasting bouquet of roses."

The $50,000 from Mrs. Carroll did arrive, and Tom was terribly excited about this magnificent gift. There is more to the story of Mrs. Carroll, and to me the fact that she is not Catholic makes the story even more beautiful.

Like most people, Tom had friendships of varying degrees. He considered one of the most disappointing consequences of public life the fact that he was not able to spend much time with friends. One of Tom's dearest friends was Sister Madeleva, who served as president of St. Mary's College in South Bend, Indiana, for 27 years. Sister Madeleva wrote nineteen books, a dozen of poetry. As a student Tom used to drop by to play the piano at St. Mary's, and Sister Madeleva always knew from a distance who the visitor was by the music that reached her ear. She wrote me once that she was pleased to have Notre Dame University close to St. Mary's as a source of dates for her girls. She also felt the ratio of the two schools was just right, approximately seven boys to each girl. In her book, *My First 70 Years*, she mentioned her friendship with Tom Dooley. Mrs. Carroll read this book, and subsequently became the largest contributor to St. Mary's, a Catholic college for women, by giving them nearly a quarter of a million dollars. Sister Madeleva died in 1964 at the age of 77. The work of Tom Dooley had many shining facets, and his spirit opened many doors.

Tom's first message from overseas on his new dictating machine started this way: "Teresa, this is the beginning of what I suppose is going to be a long friendship between you and me over this little SoundScriber. Today is the 13th of January, and at long last I am situated and settled in Muong Sing. I have a stack of mail that has come to me here of several hundred letters, and we will start to get it out. You go ahead and sign and always, of course, put secretary's initials because people will know it's not a sure thing. Just for your information, Alan Rommel and Tom Kirby are up here now. Jay Holt is here, too, a friend who is working with the Embassy for a while, the son of the Consular, and also Jerry Euster, the pilot. I feel so completely out of the picture now; all of you in the office there; my having been there for so long; all the letters being addressed to me; certain repercussions still going on, and yet I'm out here, one might say half a world away."

Tom sent back the letters he received neatly arranged in groups of 10, along with the disc which contained his replies. This made it easier to distribute work to the Disc Team. With each set he dictated a message to be inserted, indicating where he was when he dictated the letter and apologizing for not being able to send a more personal message. Tom asked me to double-space his letters to his mother so it would be easier for her to read them. I could never have anticipated the volume of work that appeared before us. Then the next day brought even more work, and I would take a quick trip at lunchtime to St. Agnes' Church and send up an SOS. "I can do all things in Him" suddenly had a new meaning.

It was at Tom's farewell party at the airport that I had met Audrey Byrne, who volunteered her services. The first night she reported for work I dictated fifty letters; when she returned them to me the next night for my signature, I knew I had struck oil, so I gave her fifty more. After this initiation, I was surprised she returned to work with me through thick and thin. Months later Tom autographed a copy of his last book to her: "To Audrey Byrne, whose typing and consequent bloody finger stumps keep my kids healthy. Tom Dooley."

A Mutual of Omaha envelope turned up in the mail one day. It was from Bob Copenhaver, dated January 15. Bob was the originator of the oft-used expression among Tom's followers: "I was a coolie for Dooley." He advised me against using form letters for any of Tom's correspondence. "Tess," he said, "if you are looking for an award around here for the 100 percent, full time, all day long, no time out, pace that you have been setting, I assure you there isn't any. That's what sort of makes a person believe that there has to be something afterwards, to make up for it." Bob's advice was always welcome. He was a man of integrity, and I was confident that with Bob and Paul Hellmuth on Tom's team, he had a strong backfield.

Although I had made my decision, as my days at Medico came to an end, I was still torn between remaining and returning to my regular job. I was so pleased to be given a luncheon by the Medico staff, where they presented me with an elegant black leather briefcase. Tom always smiled whenever he saw it; he once mentioned that it was a decided improvement over my usual shopping bag.

My arrival back on 23rd Street might be compared to a transition from city to country life. I had never realized the fast tempo of Lexington Avenue and 42nd Street before, but those twenty blocks certainly made a difference. I became an intra-city commuter, because there were trips each day to pick up or deliver Dooley mail that had to be handled. Sometimes it got so heavy, or I got so tired, that I couldn't buck the subways, and I took a cab which would leave me at the back door of the Graybar Building. I would rush up to the third floor, pick up the mail which was left in a special spot for the Disc Team, and hightail it back to my office. My cab trips were paid for by the Dr. Dooley Aid Club.

Our Disc Team continued to expand, and it was a job to keep up with their production. All finished mail came to me; I signed some letters, and others were sent to Tom for his signature. Enclosing autographs, pictures, information, sealing and stamping would occupy an entire weekend. It was expensive to mail out all the letters, but we were able to afford this, again, through the efforts of the Dooley-Aiders.

To permit Tom to see some of his mail each week, he suggested that we assign interested people the project of affixing about $2.50 worth of postage stamps to a large brown envelope, in which the letters could be forwarded to Asia. Some wonderful groups adopted this as their permanent project, and they regularly sent addressed and stamped envelopes for our use. It was wonderful to be able to send mail on to Tom without being concerned over the cost. The mail was a bond between Tom and the people interested in his work. It kept everybody united, and I believe it was well worth the expense.

Once in a while the mail would bring in special projects from Tom. He would say, "This is a project that can only go to a really good friend like the Metropolitan group, or to Agnes McShane and her group (at Borden's Company) or somebody who would be interested in doing something for Dooley personally. . . . Can you send us a couple of dozen boxes of Betty Crocker Blueberry Muffin Mix?" Somehow George Washington High School in California heard of this request and collected 3,000 boxes of muffin mix, nearly filling their gymnasium!

Paul Hellmuth was named to the Medico Planning Committee, and he agreed to work with the executive director, Dr. John Bishop, on operational and organizational problems. He set about it in his usual thorough manner, including procurement of new furniture and the promise to raise funds to pay salaries for the administrative personnel. And Paul prepared an organization chart as well. With this type of help and interest behind Medico, it seemed headed for the solid foundation that Tom wanted so much to build. The years ahead appeared very promising for this young and compassionate giant called Medico.

On his 33rd birthday, January 17, 1960, which Tom celebrated in Muong Sing, he was pensive. He felt that "it is time to admit I'm growing old." The youngsters he took time out to play with and drive around in his jeep lightened the day, but he was concerned about such things as his mail. "I hope people don't object to other people signing my mail."

About my return to the Metropolitan, Tom commented, "I think it is very significant that you go back to the Met the day after my birthday." He continued, "Sort of the end of an epoch, huh? Anyway for me. I can't thank you enough for all that you continue to do for me. I know that you understand the word 'me' is very very plural."

He began to make arrangements for Dwight and Earl to return home in April 1960, and he asked the office to be sure they received a welcome. Tom was so very grateful to them for the job they did in staying on at the hospital when he left them in August 1959 for his operation. He, himself, planned to return around May 7th for a physical check-up, "particularly a liver function test."

Tom's last book, *The Night They Burned The Mountain*, was due to come out around the 10th of May. The *Reader's Digest* condensation of the book was scheduled for their May issue, and we all eagerly looked forward to it.

Tom was known to be a very practical fellow, and he really was. He realized it might be physically impossible for him to stay another year in Laos. For this reason he appealed to Dr. Comanduras and Dr. Berman of Medico to find a replacement who would work with him for the last month before he came home and who, when Tom left, would be in charge of the hospital entirely. In the meantime, he planned to keep Muong Sing open and return from Ban Houei Sai to Muong Sing several times a week. He was enthused about the beautiful hospital site in Houei Sai, which would rest on the top of a high knoll overlooking the Mekong River. It had many advantages, the greatest of which was easy access to the river in case evacuation was necessary. With a few strokes of the paddle, one could be in Thailand. Tom worked so that everything would be set up to permit him to stay in America. As he put it, "When the doctor comes out here, I can return to America never to return to Laos, and nothing here will collapse."

On January 31st he planned to fly to Mandalay and on up to Lashio; his pilot had filed his flight plans with Rangoon. Dwight and Earl were to go along with him and spend two days at Lashio, returning to Muong Sing on February 8th. His capacity for planning always left me in a state of amazement. With all he had on his mind, he was also planning to see the authorities in South Viet Nam about setting up a Medico team there. Tom was a master when it came to understanding Asian protocol and communications, and he requested his office to notify the Lao Ambassador to the United States, Mr. C. Van Chuong, so that he, in turn, could notify the Minister of Foreign Affairs in Viet Nam of Tom's visit.

Through the efforts of friends who own a restaurant in Cleveland, we were able to secure another SoundScriber transcription machine. We now had four—two rented, one borrowed from Borden's Milk Company, and one we owned. All four were in almost constant use. Betty Moul, Kay Scanlan, and I each had one at home, and there was one at Medico's office. Most of Tom's messages came over the discs loud and clear.

"It hurts to type," Tom said, "but I enjoy answering my mail as long as we can do it on discs. I tire quickly. I get pooped by mid-afternoon; my right arm aches constantly, and when picking up a little kid and passing over a bottle of medicine, I definitely feel that the right side of me doesn't function. But I have expected that, and it doesn't bother me. The thing is to learn to get along with a right side that doesn't function. So far, so good. As for 'a little peace without pain,'" (something I had written and wished for him), "wherever I am that doesn't bother me one way or the other."

Sometimes his discs were full of jungle sounds, the hissing of a kerosene lamp, monkey chatter, or the bark of a dog. One time I saw Audrey pumping the repeat pedal over and over, and each time she listened, a big smile appeared on her face. Finally, she called me over to listen too. While Tom was dictating, he suddenly realized he had an audience of several Lao children. Calling to them in Lao and English, he asked them to come closer. There were a few words to them in Lao and then the following dialogue:

Tom: "Hip Hip!"
Children: "Hip Hip!"
Tom: "Hooray!"
Children: "Hooray!"
Tom: "Hello Secretary!"

Children: Silence, punctuated by Tom's laughter.

Tom's letters dictated on New Year's Eve were transcribed, signed, sealed, and mailed by January 12th, I was proud to report to him. I wound up my letter by telling him, "Now let me tell you there is nobody here who can ever adequately thank you for what you have done for America. You have done so much for all of us, the people that work, the people that listen, the people that read . . . None of us can thank you enough, Tom, and we will work all along the line with you." This was my promise, and with God's help I intended to keep it.

Paul Hellmuth announced his plans to visit Tom's hospital as part of a world tour in the early part of February. Before he left, he visited Tom's mother in St. Louis, who was impressed with his sincerity, ability, and his "businesslike approach" to Medico. Mrs. Dooley felt that her son was giving his life to Medico, and she longed "to see it firm and secure in the right hands." I was delighted that Paul's visit was such a success, for as far as I was concerned, every day was Thanksgiving Day as long as Paul was around.

The galley proofs of *The Night They Burned the Mountain* were en route to Tom, who was anxiously waiting their arrival, not unlike an impatient father-to-be. He had seen the jacket, a picture of himself with a Lao child, and called it "that waneful, soulful look on Dooley's face. I am not so sure it is my favorite picture, but then, of course, the pictures I like nobody else ever likes." But Mrs. Dooley's reaction was one of sadness. "It is a picture of a dying man," she told me, and it cost her tearful moments.

In the meantime, we were busy readying a bundle for Tom to be delivered by Paul Hellmuth. Muong Sing was suddenly becoming a popular visiting spot. Along with

Paul, Tom was expecting visits from Dr. Bockus, George Skakel, and *Life* people in February, and Tom had suggested that Dr. and Mrs. Commanduras come in March to inspect the two hospitals of which he was so proud.

Tom's trip to Burma was unsuccessful because he couldn't travel farther than Mandalay, due to the insurrection and rebel activities. Tom had been eager to visit Dr. Gordon Seagrave, and this was a big disappointment. But he did spend two days with Dr. Manny Voulgaropoulos in Kratie, Cambodia. "We discussed a thousand and one things. He has excellent creative ideas for new programs in Medico in the field of Cambodia, and all of them fit into our budget as I see it. However, he is going to work them out and get the okay from the Cambodian Government and present them to Paul when he gets here."

The Medico airplane made life much easier. Tom now planned to fly from Vientiane to Nam Tha to pick up the Governor and Chief Doctor and fly them to Ban Houei Sai for their first official visit. The Lao Government had finally approved "our taking over Ban Houei Sai medically." From the 13th to the 19th they planned to take gear back and forth from Muong Sing to Vientiane and to Ban Houei Sai.

While Tom was organizing things in Asia, Medico was busy organizing its Board. Tom wanted a Board that was well-informed and active. He, himself, was a master at communications and was aware of its importance. He wanted Medico to establish "auxiliaries" or "chapters" that would function in the grass roots, particularly in the towns where he spoke. A well-administered chapter would relieve the New York office of a heavy burden and relieve

Tom of fund-raising efforts. The whole burden of soliciting funds rested on his shoulders.

On February 13 he informed us there was a possibility of his getting a Congressional medal. He was "staggered," and said, "I hope I don't have to appear in person to get it . . . Do you think they can just mail it to me?" As it sadly turned out, Tom did not have to appear in Washington because President Kennedy presented it posthumously to his mother.

Now back in the Metropolitan for a month, I found myself having to think twice when I answered the telephone. "Dr. Dooley's office" was always on the tip of my tongue instead of "Mr. McGurk's office." When I told Tom my problem, he wrote: "I don't mind that, but Mr. McGurk had better not try to start practicing village medicine. *Then* I lay down the law."

Paul was due in Laos on February 20, and he was armed with a corporation presentation which he, Dr. Bishop, and the office had worked hard to complete. It set forth the whole Medico organization, complete with charts, budgets, and projected plans for the future. I knew it would do more for Tom's morale than a ton of vitamins, and I could hardly wait to hear of his reaction to it.

The Dooley-Hellmuth "summit meeting" was a success. Tom was delighted with the corporate presentation, and his voice on the disc sounded so happy: "Teresa, it is now the night of the 24th of February, about 10 P.M. Paul is sitting across from me reading a magazine, and so is Manny. They have come up to visit, and all is going very well. I met Paul in Bangkok when he arrived, and we went over and picked up Manny. We have had a couple of good days here with long talks. Paul is certainly as wonderful as you all have been telling me about, and he brought me such tremendously interesting things to read and study and talk about, although most of our discussions have been about Cambodia. We want to get things settled before Manny leaves tomorrow. First of all, before I do anything else, Paul told me to tell you that all the items you gave him were finally delivered."

Later that month the phone rang in my home about five o'clock in the morning. The operator had a long-distance call from Bangkok! I told her to hold on until I found a pencil and paper. I groped around in the darkness, and then sat down, grabbing the phone as though a weak hold on it might disconnect the call. It wasn't Tom, but his pilot, Jerry Euster. I could barely hear him. He said the 100-hour check on the plane showed that he needed several parts not available in Bangkok, and could I get them in the U.S.? With all the work and the condition of Tom's health, Jerry needed the parts as fast as he could get them and that was why he phoned. Each airplane part was Greek to me, except for "gasket." I thought desperately that if I didn't hear properly, the plane would probably never get off the ground again. So we shouted back and forth, and I can still hear Jerry saying "o" for Oscar, "a" for Alice as he spelled out each word for me. I was reduced to a wet heap by the time the phone call ended. Dawn was breaking, and I sat there looking at the list of items and wondering if I had recorded them correctly. Fortunately, before I got very far with the assignment, Tom wired that they were able to "bum the airplane parts off another Piper Apache in the area, though we have promised to replace them as soon as possible. Please send Jerry the parts-book on the airplane, because he is going to stock parts out here so that we don't have any more emergency calls." Needless to say, the parts-book went out in the next mail, posthaste. I didn't want another phone call like that in my lifetime.

The new Medico headquarters on the fourth floor was now ready for occupancy. A carpet had been donated, along with almost everything else. We were asked to keep the office plans a secret until Tom came home in May. I knew it would please him to see the new space and the new furniture. The Dooley-Aiders donated a large American flag on a stand, and Tom's gifts from Leo Cherne, the busts of Dr. Albert Schweitzer and Abraham Lincoln, were carried over the threshold and ensconced in prominent spots. The office set aside for Tom never remained exclusively his; since he was away so much, it was used by almost everyone. Someone ordered a huge box of personal stationery for Tom, but he would have no part of it, even when I suggested that he write only special letters on it.

On March 5 Tom wrote, "Many points have been worked out, and Paul and I are en route to Viet Nam to see the President about setting up a program there. We have the go-ahead from Manny for two more programs in Cambodia. On Monday we go to Viet Nam and on Wednesday Paul will head for Hong Kong and Hawaii. While in Hawaii he will see Fred Luning and the group there and work some programs out. I will return to Bangkok to pick up Georgie Skakel and Lou Werner and then return to the village. Tomorrow afternoon Dr. Ravdin and all will arrive, and I will have a program lined up for them. So we are fulfilling all obligations down here.

"Sitting at a bar last night, getting away from it all, the lady on one side of me recognized me and passed me a check for $500! The moral of this memorandum: Dooley should sit in bars more often."

Paul arrived home after St. Patrick's Day, and we arranged to meet at the Beekman Towers. My prized possessions number very few items, but one of them is a ring that Paul brought back with him. The card, in Tom's writing and signed by Tom and Paul, read "A Princess Ring for a Princess." A Princess Ring is made of semi-precious stones grouped in the shape of a Buddhist temple. You can unscrew the top and replace it with another, to complement the dress you are wearing, from a supply of ring tops in stones of various colors. I think the card means almost more to me than the ring.

Paul and I talked at length. Medico was having problems in adjusting to its growth. There were difficulties and slowness in shipping the personal effects of the new doctors, the drug shipments were late, and no action had been taken on the brochure Tom wanted. There just seemed to be no end to the problems. As Mrs. Dooley often said, "The field can only be as good as the home office makes it." Without proper administration on the home front, obviously the field would suffer.

I was delighted to hear Paul say that his visit with Tom convinced him that all the good things he had heard about Tom were true. He saw a Tom he had never known, and saw him at his best, a jungle doctor in action. As Paul continued his report, he told me of the affection the children in Madam Ngai's orphanage had for Tom, particularly the child who was left to die. In one of Tom's KMOX broadcasts, he told the story of this child:

"The little boy, a hunchback whose spine was deformed by tuberculosis, and to whom I gave streptomycin for 37 days and nights, came out to see me. This was the little child we found abandoned, sickened unto death. The communists had abandoned him right on the frontier line, near the village of Haiphong (Viet Nam). When we found him, the whole back portion of his scalp had been gnawed away, as though rats had chewn on his scalp. I saw that he's a fine little fellow now. He's bald and always shall be, because no hair will ever grow on his scar tissue. But he's alive and he smiles and he lives in freedom."

Paul told me how lettuce in Tom's hospital compound was treated with iodine and water, and turned a shade of brown before it could be safely eaten. As for Tom's energy, despite his letters claiming he was getting old, Paul reported that Tom led them all a merry chase. Tom's faith, his sensitivity, and his kindness were all attested to by Paul, who observed them at first-hand. I always felt there was in Tom a humility that he wanted to keep, but at the same time, knowing he had a job to do, he always did it even if he had to talk from house tops to get his message across. It meant that much to him, and it was sometimes misunderstood. As a lawyer, Paul came in contact with all types of people and I have always felt that lawyers, like priests, are good judges of people. It was good to know that Paul found these wonderful things to report about Tom.

CARE pointed out to Tom that for the first time in Viet Nam's history the country had made one of the finest contracts with Americans, the one for Tom's new hospital in the province of Quang Ngai. The Viet Minh took over Quang Ngai when France returned to establish colonial rule, and the province never returned to the hands of the French. It was run by the communists from 1946 until 1954, at which time the Geneva Treaty was signed. As it fell below the 17th parallel, the province came under the rule of the South Vietnamese. A few Viet Minh soldiers left, but most of them merely took off their uniforms and returned to their rice paddies. Therefore, this territory was "hot" politically, one where there was a tremendous amount of procommunist activity. President Diem said that he hoped that the presence of the Americans in Tom's new hospital in Quang Ngai would reassure the people that Americans are not the monsters that they had been made out to be. He also hoped that their presence in a Vietnamese provincial hospital would enhance the villager's confidence and faith in their own Vietnamese government. Quang Ngai had approximately 700,000 inhabitants and about 20,000 mountain tribes. This would be the *only* hospital for the whole province, with about 200 to 250 beds. Tom hoped that the New York office would expedite the drug shipments to Quang Ngai, and he was annoyed at this date to realize that the drugs he had chosen in December in the warehouse in New York had not as yet arrived in Laos, and it was almost spring. Tom said, "The whole superstructure of Medico *exists* for this type of work."

Among his other responsibilities, Tom had to negotiate with foreign governments and succeed in getting the best terms possible for the medical teams about to settle there. Then such things as stoves, ice boxes, furniture, drugs, equipment, and the attendant shipment problems came next in order. But Tom had ability, and he used every bit of it in arranging for everything down to the smallest detail. He knew from experience what they needed, and he saw that they got it.

At 11 P.M. on St. Patrick's Day Tom wrote that his heart

was set on getting Quang Ngai staffed, and that he also had a project in Malaya fermenting. Since New York had not come up with a medical replacement, Tom took steps and on his own had the good fortune to find Dr. Richard Hauptman, a 70-year old doctor of Viennese birth. Tom called him "extremely gentle and a man of great simplicity."

About his return to America, Tom wrote, "Even when I am home, I must continue to serve these people out here by utilizing every inch and moment of my time to the best advantage, and by the best means make my natural contributions to Medico. Everything else, my personal health, etc., must come second to these things." Speaking of the hospital compound he was preparing to leave, Tom confided to his mother that it was difficult to turn over "all the things that I have built, the small table in front of me, my metal stationery box, my filing cabinet, the 'Route 66' pillow, and everything else . . . but I must not become too strongly attached to these physical things. The spirit of my hospital will continue whether I am here or not, of this I am sure."

Muong Sing buzzed with a well-kept secret. Tom had arranged for an award to be presented to Dwight and Earl by the King of Laos. On receiving the King's concurrence, Tom was overjoyed. Dwight and Earl were the second and third foreigners in the history of the country to be given the award, the Order of the Million Elephants and the White Parasol. Tom had been the first.

On March 22 I sat bolt upright in the subway as I read in a New York newspaper that the students of the John Philip Sousa Junior High School had written to Eisenhower, Khrushchev, Macmillan, Nehru, and Tom Dooley asking them to comment on the problem of peace for their yearbook. The paper said that only Khrushchev had replied, after he had sent representatives to the school to check it all out. The main point of the story was that no one else took the time to answer the student's letter. As Tom's secretary I was frantic, wondering if we had lost the letter, or perhaps hadn't yet forwarded it to Tom in Asia. I could hardly wait to get home and get a note off to Tom, asking him if he had seen the letter. I need not have done so, because the very next day the mail we received contained Tom's answer to the students. They later printed Tom's letter in their yearbook and Khrushchev's did not appear. Strangely enough, none of the newspapers reported Tom's reply. I am happy to give it here in full:

March 31, 1960

John Philip Sousa Junior High School
c/o Miss Lucille Di Domenico
1914 Bussing Avenue
New York 66, New York

Dear Editorial Board of *The Blue and Gray:*

It is very kind of you to ask Tom Dooley to write a letter to all of you. I am, indeed, honored.

As you read this letter, you sit in the civilized world. I live in the world beyond. More than mere miles separate us. At home in America, you have all the comforts of health and happiness and security. Here in the high valley of Northern Laos, in these stark, hot hills of Asia, people are born darkly, they live darkly, they die darkly. Even though the colors of the streaming sky at sunset are staggering; even though the rose and purple are soft and they flow on the faces of our people with gentleness . . . nevertheless, this part of Asia is raw and naked and ugly. The people are wretched and sick and they lack so very, very much.

A challenge is flung to all of us who are born in freedom, freedom from pain and freedom from want. The world in Asia is one great groan of agony. The world in America is one great island of comfort.

The best way to bridge this gap between peoples is with the powerful thing called love . . . and the action that love produces. This action can be in the form of help to medicine, help to education, help through money, or help through simple understanding. But all these things are predicated on *knowledge* of the need.

I urge all of you at John Philip Sousa Junior High to become aware of the needs that exist in the world. Project yourselves beyond your campus, your continent, and your customs. Look at the simple humanity of the world . . . and listen to its cry.

Seek a channel to be of service to the people who "ain't got it so good." Search for some investment of your humanity. Find a way to invest a chunk of your life for the people over here. If you do, you will know the sweetness of achievement, and the quiet glow of happiness that comes in the heart.

Your book is dedicated to Dr. Albert Schweitzer. Dr. Schweitzer is the man who has given direction to my life. May I pass on to you the words that Dr. Schweitzer told me many, many years ago around the dining room table at Lambarene: "I don't know what your destiny will ever be, but this I do know . . . you shall always have happiness if you seek and find how to serve."

He later sent this message to all of the doctors of Medico . . . and I pass it on to all of you reading *The Blue and Gray:*

"Learn that the most powerful instrument in the arms of today is love . . . love among all men."

Again, my very best wishes to all the graduating class, and the students who are coming up the line. Best wishes from half a world away.

> Very sincerely,
>
> THOMAS A. DOOLEY, M.D.

Every once in a while we had a glow of satisfaction over our small part in Tom's work, such as when Mutual of Omaha ran the "Keep Talking Show." At the end of the program the master of ceremonies mentioned that he had telephoned Dr. Tom Dooley's mother to find out how Tom was feeling, and she said she had a letter from Tom just that morning. Consequently, she was able to give him up-to-the-minute details about how Tom was doing. Having transcribed that letter from Tom and forwarded it to Mrs. Dooley, we got quite a thrill behind the scenes.

One of Tom's dear friends was Sister Mary Brigid of St. Vincent's Charity Hospital in Cleveland, Ohio. When Sister was in New York, Kay and I met her and Sister Agnes Ann for dinner, and Sister Mary Brigid enthralled us with stories of Tom's days in the Cleveland hospital as a young intern. "He always was concerned for the sick children," she recalled. "On days off he would bring his car to the hospital and take the sickliest or least attractive youngsters for a day's outing. The kids would return with balls, pandas, balloons, and stars in their eyes after a typical Dooley outing."

Tom's enthusiasm for making KMOX tapes began to wane as his and other problems increased and his health declined. Sometimes he had two tapes to make in one night, but since he had promised Bob Hyland and his friends in St. Louis, and since the listeners looked forward to hearing, "Hello, this is Tom Dooley from half a world away," he stuck with it.

The end of March brought exciting news to the sleepy village of Muong Sing. A wire crackled over the cables, addressed to Dr. Tom Dooley: "If convenient and desirable, will happily fly Bangkok then Vientiane. Cable best day. Regards. Arthur Godfrey." Tom was elated. On the 2nd of April Tom was in Vientiane, waiting for Mr. Godfrey, who was due on the 3rd. As Tom wrote, "We had quite a fabulous time." Arthur Godfrey made a recording of his interview with Tom, and played it over CBS radio on April 12. One of the stories that particularly amused Mr. Godfrey involved the only two jeeps in that whole area of Laos. The driver of Tom's jeep was so surprised to encounter another jeep on the road that, in his shock and amazement, he ran into it!

Arthur Godfrey left Muong Sing for Bangkok on April 7th, and Tom began to plan his return home in only four more weeks. The *Life* magazine reporter had just left, and Tom was concerned over the way the article might turn out. The reporter had just finished a story on Prime Minister Sarit and had come up to Muong Sing as angry as if "he had been gnawing on bark all day. With this attitude, he then spent some time with me." Tom was sure at this stage that the article would be anything but a "God bless" type. The *Life* article came out before Easter, and it was vitriolic. I was concerned about Tom's reaction, and felt badly, but I need not have done so. After his return to America, when someone mentioned the *Life* article at a press conference, Tom paraphrased an old Chinese saying: "Man who lift head above crowd bound to get hit with rotten fruit."

Dwight and Earl left on April first for the U.S. and Tom wondered if the new team would measure up to the "smooth sophistication and inner qualities of philosophy" that he thought Dwight and Earl possessed. The acceptance of his plans for a hospital in Malaya by the Medico office in New York made Tom very happy. He now had hospitals in Laos, Kratie, Quang Ngai, Haiti, Kuala Lumpur, and Afghanistan.

Chapter IX

TOM'S SPEECH: "THE
HUMANITY OF MAN"

When the condensation of Tom's new book, *The Night
They Burned the Mountain,* appeared in *Reader's Digest*
that April, people began writing to me at my office since
Tom gave my address in the book. In one letter a mid-
western woman offered to help Tom by rubbing his back;
another woman wrote me and offered to rub my face with
avocado cold cream. We both appreciated the good intentions, but declined the honors.

The Reader's Digest condensation also did wonders for
contributions, and we had more than 200 pieces of mail
every day in the period following publication in the magazine. The girls handling "projects," under the supervision
of Edna Fannon, were busier than ever. As requests came
in from Tom, the girls assigned these projects to the
people who offered their help. The projects ranged from
children's sweaters and blankets to suction machines and
tires for the airplane. The beautiful letters from generous
people who wanted to give Tom a helping hand were, to
me, one of the biggest "fringe benefits" of my work.

When it came time to set up a new budget, Alexander Smith of the accounting division of the Metropolitan Life Insurance Company offered his services to Dr. John Bishop, executive director of Medico. (Dr. Bishop has been a member of the New York Chapter's Board of Trustees since its inception.) Tom's tribute in *The Night They Burned the Mountain* to the employees of my company, for the help they had given him, was the talk of the Metropolitan officers. Tom sent an autographed advance copy of his new book to my boss, James E. McGurk, at his home in Pleasantville, and he received it there on Easter morning. He wrote to Tom in Rome, expressing his gratitude and reminiscing a bit: "I shall never forget the day you came into the office to ask us for Miss Gallagher . . . I know I am only one of millions who couldn't say 'no' to you."

A charming story came to us in the mail from Nettie's Flower Shop in St. Louis. Paul, the six-year old son of one of Nettie's employees, was on his way to Sunday School when his mother told him she had named him after St. Paul, the great missionary. Paul thought about this for a moment and then asked, "Was St. Paul as good as Dr. Dooley?"

A UPI release out of Bangkok shortly after Tom left for Rome caught our attention. Tom was quoted as saying, "My head tells me I should stay in America, and my heart says I will be back in June."

It was comforting to hear from an old friend like Sister Mary Corinne, O.P., a teacher, who told us how Tom had made a marked impression on the life of a young student. She added, "And he has done so on many young people. He is a shining light in this sad, disillusioned world and an inspiration to young and old." I received another such lift in the form of a lovely book of poems by Khamchan Pradith, of the Royal Embassy of Laos, who later went to the UN. The book was beautifully inscribed "To Miss Teresa Gallagher, who shares with Dr. Tom, his team and Medico, the worries and the quiet triumphs of my people and other lands."

The spring of 1960 saw Tom more worried about Medico's future than he was about his illness. Flying over Malaya on the 27th of April he wrote that he was "coming home with 'warpaint' on . . . I intend to give that place the strong leadership it needs," he said. "Mail will continue to be answered by the volunteers. I'll organize it as soon as I get home and hold one large volunteer meeting. I know this puts you in a tenuous position, but you are with me and I'm Medico." Tom planned to have the volunteers answer the mail personally, without going "through channels." I was concerned that I would be infringing on Medico's paid staff, but Tom quickly put my fears to rest by saying, "Anything concerning TAD personally is your business. I've made it so." While it was gratifying to know that he had faith and trust in me, I was astounded.

At this early date Tom was jokingly planting the idea of my writing a book. His suggested title for me was, "I Went Around the World on a SoundScriber." With Tom due in May, Paul Hellmuth approached me with the idea of requesting a three-week leave of absence. I had only been back to work about three months, and I was reluctant to press my luck and ask for more favors from my boss. I told Paul I would see what kind of a solution I could work out, and I estimated what would happen financially, if I were to resign at this time and work full-time for Tom. In doing so, I would be eligible for a modified retirement. I decided to write down on a sheet of paper all the reasons, pro and con, for giving up my job. I was on retreat when I did this, and I prayed hard for the right answer; when I left the confines of the convent, I had come to the conclusion that I had but one choice: to stay and work for the Metropolitan and give Tom all the spare time I had, including my vacation time. With the help of the volunteers, I thought this would work out.

Before returning to America, Tom suggested to Medico that his brother Malcolm come to work for them. The idea was submitted for the approval of the executive committee, and they agreed. Malcolm resigned his job in Detroit and moved his family to Huntington, Long Island, accepting the position of Executive Director of Medico.

In the meantime, Tom's stopover in Rome permitted him to visit with his dear friends, Lorraine and Kevin Brennan. Paul, in Europe on a business trip, made arrangements to meet Tom in Rome and fly back home with him. The plane from Europe was fogbound over New York, and Tom and Paul found themselves landing in Chicago, facing an overnight delay. Tom then surprised his brother Malcolm in Detroit by telephoning him from the airport. The next day, en route to New York, accompanied now by Paul and Malcolm, Tom worked on the speech he was to give that evening at the annual dinner of the Medical Society of the State of New York at the Hotel Pierre.

Since it was a weekday, I took a vacation day and had the usual "office" set up in his hotel room with typewriter, stationery, and the rest. I wondered whether his illness would have affected his appearance. Tom burst into the hotel room his usual good-looking, good-natured, cheerful self, and all my fears disappeared. He presented me with a straw, leather-lined bag with brass handles and crest, "a little gift from Rome." My leather briefcase, a gift from the office staff, was already showing signs of wear from the terrible beatings it took, and the new bag was a welcome replacement. I gave Tom all the phone messages that had accumulated from family, friends, press, radio and television. While Tom answered some of his calls, I began typing his speech from the cards he had prepared in flight.

A press conference was held at the Waldorf at 11:00 A.M. and the press turned out en masse. After the press conference, he made a tape for the Dave Garroway show. After his big speech at the Hotel Pierre in the evening, he was to go on the Jack Paar Show at 11 P.M.

Thus Tom's first day in New York was just as hectic and crowded as I had anticipated. He ran into only one minor crisis. En route to the Pierre, he realized he wasn't wearing a cummerbund, so I hopped out of the cab, rushed to a store on Madison Avenue to buy one, and hurried back to the Pierre lobby to catch up with him.

The speech he gave that night was, I thought, one of the best he ever delivered. It was a detailed, eloquent and moving statement of his own concept of person-to-person medical work abroad. Though it was delivered to a critical audience of physicians, the members of the Medical Society of the State of New York, it was very well received and warmly applauded. It was later reprinted in one of the medical journals, and Tom gave it the title, "The Humanity of Man." I think this last formal public statement of his, one of the lengthiest yet one of the most readable, deserves to be reprinted here in full:

This generation of physicians, more than any other, must demonstrate the spirit of love for mankind that is strong enough to answer the challenge of hate in most of the world today.

I just left an area where the challenge was a palpable, demonstrable thing—a very living thing, and its challenge is yours and mine.

There is a statement Toynbee recently made that "our age will be remembered not for its horrifying crimes, nor for its astonishing inventions, but because it is the first age since the dawn of history that dared to be practical, to make the benefits of civilization available to the whole human race." The benefits of our civilization are available to the whole human race. This is the accomplishment of our decade.

I am sure you know the medical statistics as well as I— two-thirds of the human race, two-thirds of all the men that God has put on this earth, have absolutely no adequate medical care available, and one-half of them are born darkly, they live darkly, and they die darkly—without ever seeing a physician. While you and I enjoy our meal here, it is an absolute statistic that tonight over half the people on earth will go to bed just a little hungry.

This is bad enough, but now these people are maturing, and now they are becoming convinced that their plight is not inevitable. I live among that half; I walk with their kings and with their prime ministers; I deliver their children in wretched, smoky huts in their mountains. Among these people there is a strong, palpable surging, a stirring among the intellectual elite, like the students in my village, the young functionaires, the village chieftains—even among the refugees there is a stirring. These people of Asia and of Africa are seeking their place in the growing village, their place in their newly-independent nations, their place in the world. Their place beneath the self-same sky and sun that we have here in Manhattan. These people have bitterness; they have bad memories; they have confusion; and they have much of the rightful resentment of a formerly oppressed people. Sure, they make mistakes—they stir aimlessly many times. But these people, this half of the earth, these people are determined to find their place beneath the world sun. Among them—no, with them—we must work.

Okay—that's admitted. But what of the why, and the who, and the how of working with these people. Why must we work, you and me? Who must work? How must we work? To tell you why we must work I would just reiterate what you already know. But then the ear oftentimes yearns to hear what the heart knows. I believe that there rests upon the individual citizen of our country the responsibility for America. And on America rests the major part of the responsibility of the world for all men. I believe that each citizen of America, each you and me, is America. America isn't a small body of men in Washington. America isn't a small group of men in power—America is you and me—and accordingly what you and I do is always and forever and in every way important to America. And accordingly to the world.

We believe that the highest purpose of man is liberation from the bonds of fear, of human degradation, and of poverty and of misery. You and I must liberate people from the bonds of pain. There is the whole—you and I. We must do this because we have been given the faint breath of talent as doctors. You and I can fulfill this highest purpose of man, this liberation. We can do it with vigor and vitality, and we shall do it. It is you and I in the field of medicine who can best utilize two weapons—the weapon of compassion and the weapon of kindness. These weapons strengthen themselves, because when they are used they call forth an answering kindness. If you use the weapon of hate, you get hate for a response. If you use the weapon of kindness, you get for your response kindness.

It is therefore the furthest reaching and the most effective of all forces; and you and I as doctors in the free world can best utilize this weapon. And we will, because we are deeply involved in the destinies of all men everywhere.

Medicine is unique because it is above the give and take of national rivalries. Medicine is not touched by politics; medicine is not touched by the sharp edges of clashing principles; medicine is not involved in the soft, gummy compromises and compromising that so often must be done.

Let's get practical now. How do we do it? How do we implement this high purpose? We all know that it is more blessed to give than to receive, and we all know also that it is a damn sight more difficult. To implement this we in the free world established institutions. Medico has for its purpose a very simple aim—we want to take care of people who are sick. We want to practice medicine—the simple art of helping people who are sick because they are sick. We want our medicine not to be a tool of foreign policy and not to be a medium of evangelism. Honorable as these two things might be, we want our medicine not to interfere with the nationalism of new nations because, as a Negro doctor in Kenya told me four days ago, "Nationalism is the aspiration of people who want to be themselves. Medicine does not affect this nationalism."

Tom's Speech: "The Humanity of Man"

There are many institutions besides Medico working in this field. None of these institutions is in competition with each other or repeats any other, contrary to a lot of public opinion. Every institution in the field of medicine in foreign lands has its own sphere of activity. Some are on a larger scale; some are involved in teaching, some in preventive medicine. The institutions like the International Cooperations Administration, the World Health Organization, the Hope Ship, the Pan American Union, the Columbo Plan—each of these is in its sphere of activity and nobody is in competition with anybody. These organizations, however, are involved basically in the field of prevention and in the field of teaching. Medico, in this family of international medicine, is the country doctor.

How do we work in Medico? We believe very strongly that there is one unique essence that we possess; we believe that the essential instrument for good in the world is the human spirit. Our x-ray machines and our diagnostic acumen and our hospitals and some of their magnificent air-conditioned splendor are fine indeed. But the essential instrument for good, the basic component for a physician, is the instrument of his human spirit, the instrument of his compassion, the instrument of his love.

Let this human spirit of an American work side by side with this human spirit of an Asian, or of an African. It does no good whatsoever to construct a foundation, or to build a building, or to launch a ship, or to establish a foundation, or to manufacture any kind of program if you do not seek and utilize to its utmost the elements of the human heart and the human spirit.

Medico now, after only a little more than two years of existence, has the following programs. We have a Cambodian Hospital, run by Dr. Manny Voulgaropoulos, and we have a new hospital being built in Cambodia in the town of Atana, Sukari. We have a team in Vietnam, a surgical team that worked there and that has now departed. We have a new hospital that is being built by the Vietnamese government and we provide medical services for the largest orphanage in Saigon.

In Laos we have just built a new village hospital in a town called Ban Houei Sai, and, as perhaps you know, Dooley has a small, little hut of a hospital in a town that quivers on the frontier, a town called Muong Sing.

In Malaya we have just signed an accord with the Malayan government to dispatch a team to Kuala Lampur next month. In Kenya, we have a young Kikuku doctor whose name is Dr. Mungai Njoroge who is doing an excellent job, and we have just pledged him a $25,000 new clinic which will go into construction immediately. One of our largest is a medical service program in Haiti, working with Johns Hopkins University and the Henry Ford Hospital. We have teams or support programs in Gabon, in Peru, in Jordan, in Afghanistan, and other projects around the world.

These are not plans and programs in blueprints; these are existing programs. They are there now and a few of these who do not have their staffs will have a staff very soon.

These are simple programs. The global planners are indubitably scoffing at us and I couldn't care less. These programs each have satellite activity around them, the simple village hospital with a half dozen clinics in the mountains around it. But each team is an intimate part of the village life; each team doctor goes to the weddings and goes to the funerals. Each team doctor is a part of that community life. We don't come in, spend a few weeks and then pull out— we are part of that community life. And because this idea has become beloved in Asia, the host governments put up what we need. The host governments pay all indigenous salaries; they build the buildings and give us warehousing and internal transportation and a *carte blanche* for their medicines. Medico is not a charity organization. The oft-repeated truth that I feel so strongly as all of us in Medico do, is that unlimited charity or the unlimited giving away of things can rob a man, and perhaps a nation, of his self-respect.

The drugs that are given us for our projects are donated by the drug companies of America. The surgical supply houses donate all of the surgical supplies and equipment we need. We have plenty of volunteer doctors and nurses. The money is donated to us by people in America.

All donated money that has been given to us by all of you —every single dollar that is donated sends 100 cents to our overseas projects. The administration of our offices, the payment of our salaries for the people here in New York City— is entirely and totally covered by the royalties of a specific author we won't name. Anyway, as long as you keep buying my books, it keeps paying for the overhead, and therefore every donated dollar takes care of my kids.

A question is always asked of those who go out in the world and leave behind them certain accoutrements of civilization. That question is, "Okay, buddy, what do you get out of it?" Well, ladies and gentlemen, I can speak for all of these young doctors—because I've been in this business of village medicine for six years—and I'll tell you what I get out of it. I get plenty. All of us have the same quiet, inner joy that you have when you see your patients' eyes light up just a little bit because of you. But take that patient and put him in a hospital, in a high mountain valley, half a world away, where without you he has black magic or sorcery; you heal him and the glow inside of you is a wonderful thing, a thing that is full of wonder. We who are in this field have formed a new purpose and a new order in our lives. And we have a fulfillment of man's appetite, the normal appetite for fruitful activity and a high quality of life.

We have the satisfaction of doing a job that needs doing—not by a government—but needs doing by individuals, by Americans. We have that feeling of accomplishment. We are trying to make the world just a little better, bit by bit, and little by little.

We feel good in our hearts when we know that we are giving meaning to the fundamental yearning of all men in all lands everywhere. And I've seen this yearning in many men, in many lands, many times. And that is a fundamental yearning—to be of service to somebody else, to help somebody who "ain't got it so good," in our case by utilizing this wonderful weapon of medicine blended with compassion.

But our deepest reward is knowing that we of Medico in some small way are helping to fulfill a dream—a dream that a young Jewish girl wrote of in the furor of World War II. We feel as though we are somehow or other helping to bring into being the words of the dream of Anne Frank: "People will change and men will become good again. And these pitiless days will come to an end, and the world will know once again, order, rest, and peace."

Tom's speaking tour around the country started off badly; in Lubbock, Texas, he got a sore throat, and autographing sessions seemed endless. But Tom never protested and his throat soon improved. At the same time, Earl Rhine was making an appearance at a high school in Austin, begging help for their work. Tom next spoke in

Dallas, to the Health Insurance Association of America. Then he appeared at St. Mary's College in South Bend, Indiana; at Catholic Central High School in Springfield, Ohio; and at the San Francisco Opera House, after receiving the keys to the city of San Francisco. He toured Santa Clara and Los Angeles, where he spoke in the Shrine Auditorium. After talking at Immaculate Heart College in Hollywood, he had lunch with Martin Manulus, producer at 20th Century-Fox. Then he flew back to Milwaukee, where he addressed the Catholic Hospital Association of the United States and Canada. On June 3 he spoke at Finch College in New York, and on June 5 he was awarded an honorary degree by Notre Dame. Two other distinguished guests on that occasion were President Eisenhower and Cardinal Montini who later became Pope Paul VI.

He was the guest of the National Press Club on June 8. The club consists of most Washington correspondents attached to leading dailies throughout the country, of a large number of foreign correspondents headquartered in Washington, the top staff members of press services, and public relations men and business consultants who previously were newspaper people. Membership is limited to men, and a normal turnout for a luncheon discussion is from 100 to 400 members, depending upon the prominence of the speaker and his potential for making news. Some of Tom's predecessors at the NPC included Anthony Eden, Harold Macmillan, Henry Cabot Lodge, Adlai Stevenson, and Nikita Khrushchev. The speaker was expected to make news of a "general interest nature," field questions, and toss back answers to give them material for a story or information for their files. Tom was at home with this group of good-natured men who enjoyed his good humor and wit.

Tom was tired of hotel life and its lack of privacy, particularly since he wasn't feeling good, and he asked Kay and me to find him an apartment in New York. Tom told me that he had an apartment in Washington, D. C., in which he had hoped to hang up his shingle. It had been completely furnished at the time his book *Deliver Us from Evil* made the best-seller list, and his mother had just put up the drapes when Tom announced he was returning to Laos.

The remainder of June found Tom speaking at Annapolis and St. John's College in Baltimore, to the Baltimore Junior League, and to the youngsters at Buckeye Boys State in Ohio. Then he was off to Sandusky High, Boston College, Pittsfield College, and Holy Cross. On June 20 Tom appeared as the number two speaker at the National Jay Cee's Convention, the keynoter being Vice President Nixon. Tom took time out to attend the wedding of Bart Hogan, the Surgeon General's son, and he escorted his "very favorite female," Clare Murphy, to the wedding.

While Tom was lecturing in the States, Dr. Hauptman was holding sick call at Muong Sing, aided by Tom Kirby. At Ban Houei Sai, Alan Rommel and John Kim were putting the finishing touches on the hospital. Tom Kirby wrote to tell us that Tom had brought a record player for the team, and they wanted some records. We assigned this project to those who would know more about the tastes of young people in music than we did.

A contingent of doctors and aides was ready to take off for various hospitals under the aegis of Medico. A farewell party was given for them at the Waldorf, and Tom briefed them on what they could expect. His discussion ranged from customs surrounding the birth of a baby to the effect of evil spirits on the life and death of a patient. I sat in on this briefing, and I did not envy the tough job that confronted all of them.

Before he left the States, Tom wanted to buy Malcolm a birthday present. He had in mind a map of the world that would cover one wall of Malcolm's office. Tom explained how he wanted to differentiate his various hospital programs, with different colors for permanent programs and for support programs. What he wanted was something that would help Malcolm to locate the hospital programs, in relation to other parts of the world, at a glance. We were in the vicinity of the office in the Graybar Building. Pressed for time, Tom was torn between getting back to the office and taking time out to shop for Malcolm's gift. I suggested that since we weren't too far from the map store, why didn't he follow through with his idea now? Tom reluctantly agreed, and once in the store quickly started looking over their maps, and it was obvious that he enjoyed this kind of shopping. He left the salesman far behind as he selected the various sections of maps to be placed side by side to form a map of the world. I was impressed with the ease with which he did this. When we left the store, the purchase made, Tom turned and said, very seriously, "Teresa, you're the only one who has ever been able to make me change my mind."

I was very surprised since I was not aware I had attempted to do so. We approached Fifth Avenue, and Tom was still very serious. As we crossed the street, he took my hand and said, "No man is a hero to his valet, Teresa." I was so concerned over the traffic that I was unable to reply that this hero would always remain a hero to me. And then

Tom expressed his gratitude and feelings about our association. I continued to marvel to myself that he felt I had succeeded in changing his mind, because I knew too well that Tom always called the shots. I do recall that the gravity with which he spoke that day amazed me.

On June 23, 1960, Henry Cabot Lodge, U.S. Ambassador to the United Nations, spoke of Tom at a tribute dinner in these words: "The work which Dr. Dooley is doing has struck a loud, responsive chord among Americans. He has appealed to what Lincoln called 'the better angels of our nature,' our compassion and our generous concern for our fellow man. His shining example, this talent for expressing himself in words, and his organizing powers have brought forth a response of action and sacrifice in the shape of the Medico program which is truly a model for practical humanitarians. One moral of this is clear. Contrary to the lamentations which we sometimes hear, the American people in their prosperity have not grown fat and flabby. They have not lost their souls. There are countless Americans who try to live up to the Biblical saying that 'to whom much is given, of him will much be required.' Those good people are the strength of our nation.

"Whoever works for the United States in this dangerous era, especially in the field of foreign affairs, feels what a precious asset Dr. Dooley is to our cause. Whether he means to be or not, he is a devastating argument against the forces that wish to destroy our good name in the world as a part of their strategy of conquest. In fact, one feels that if there were an unlimited number of Dr. Dooleys, this country would have no foreign relations problems at all.

"In particular Americans have, from the beginning of

our history to the present day, a tradition of pioneer neighborliness, of helping people because we like them. Dr. Dooley symbolizes that tradition. If we lived up to it all around the world, many of our worries would fall away. But he is more than a fighter in our cause. In a deeper sense the quality of courageous compassion which he typifies really *is* our cause. It is very close to the heart of the matter. It is not a means to an end but an end in itself. It is one of the highest virtues of which a free man is capable.

"We who are engaged in the long struggle against communism do not believe in struggle for its own sake or in power for its own sake. Our efforts are expended and our risks are run because we know that behind the ramparts there is something which we and the great majority of humanity think is worth saving. The essence of that something is freedom, and at the heart of freedom is the fire of compassion and service which burns in free men like Dr. Tom Dooley.

"Let every American home share that inner fire; then surely our cause will win in the end because it will deserve to win."

Tom arranged for Bob Copenhaver and Malcolm to visit his hospitals overseas, and the trip was scheduled for around Election Day. The first I head of these plans was in Dr. McNeer's office on Thursday, June 30. Tom was sitting on a table, Gandhi-fashion, with a sheet around him, waiting for a check-up by Dr. McNeer. He had called me in as he waited for the doctor, and this was indeed a new setup for me. I sat on a low stool at the head of the examining table, and Tom peered down from above as he dictated memos to the office and letters to the teams. When the doctor came in, I quickly exited. Dr. McNeer offered me the use of a desk in another office, so I was able to complete some work. When the check-up was over, we packed up our papers, closed our briefcases, and took off. When I asked how Dr. McNeer thought things were, Tom said, "Negative, but a few lumps in the liver." He didn't sound concerned; and that word "negative" was good news to me. He spent that evening with his mother and some friends.

Tom's departure in early July was no more orderly than the previous ones. This time we were all "chasing" Tom through the huge parking lots because, having eaten dinner at the airport, we found there was no vehicle to get us from one side of the airport to the other. We were barely able to wave goodbye to Tom as he boarded the flight. Malcolm, like the rest of us, was exhausted from the race. He stood very tall in front of us wilting females, raised his handkerchief over his head like a travel guide for a group tour, and we followed him single file out of the congested airport. On reflection, I thought Tom perhaps planned it that way to avoid any sad goodbyes.

The unbelievable score for this visit home for Tom was 55 speeches in 39 cities in 36 days. In Laos he now had 6 team members; in Cambodia 11; in Viet Nam 5; in Malaya 5; in Haiti 6; in Peru 2; in Afghanistan 3; and Tanganyika 2. For a fellow recuperating from a serious operation and a skin graft, this was a fantastic convalescence. The mail these days was different, too; people sending in contributions told Tom they hoped he would rest and take care of himself.

In Hawaii Tom prepared a speech to be given in Tokyo. He was to address the Zen Zenkuren, whose demonstrations had just given President Eisenhower such a hard time. Tom tried out his speech on a little Japanese maid at the hotel in Hawaii, and she understood his Japanese very well. When Tom arrived in Tokyo on the 19th, he was given a standing ovation by the Zen Zenkuren. The Jesuit fathers at Sophia University were also delighted with his talk. On the 23rd of July Tom flew to Hong Kong, then took off for Bangkok, remaining there until the second of August. He planned to be back in Muong Sing by the fourth.

As Tom winged his way to Tokyo on his way "home" to Muong Sing, he wrote me one of the most beautiful tributes a gal could ever get in a lifetime:

Dear Tess:

Eight hours ago I left Hawaii; in two more hours I'll be in Tokyo. I am truly apprehensive. I have been practising my speech with the Japanese maid at the Reef—so far so good. Mount Fujiyama just came in view . . . all snow-capped, serene, and majestic. So many many thanks to you, Teresa, for the time and effort and sweat and love you have given to me and mine. You give of yourself, and this is something beyond gadgets, money, or time. When I'm home I crave a spiritual sharing of what I am trying to carry on and teach and do. You share this spiritual, tender touching thing with me. Many many thanks. Fuji off the wing tip. . . . Asia beneath me once again . . . I'm home!

Much much love always,

Tom

After reading and re-reading Tom's beautiful message from the shadow of Fujiyama, I sent him a copy of a prayer I kept on my calendar. All of a sudden this prayer took on new meaning for me these days, and I found it very consoling. As I got more involved with Tom's work I seemed to find great solace in its delicate and wise wording. It was composed by Cardinal Newman:

"God has created me to do Him some definite service; He has committed some work to me which He has not committed to another; I have my mission—I may never know it in this life, but I shall be told it in the next. I am a link in a chain, a bond of connection between persons. He has created me for naught; I shall do good, I shall do His work; I shall be an angel of peace, a preacher of truth in my own place while not intending it, if I do but keep His commandments.

"Therefore, I will trust Him whatever, wherever I am. I can never be thrown away. If I am in sickness, my sickness will serve Him. In perplexity, my perplexity may serve Him, if I am in sorrow, my sorrow may serve Him. He does nothing in vain. He knows what He is about. He may take away my friends. He may throw me among strangers. He may make me feel desolate, make my spirits sink, hide my future from me . . . still He knows what He is about."

As I wrote to Tom at this time, "There is no explanation for the strong desire I have to help you, and the fear when I get tired that I might not be able to. You know, you've said it so many times: 'The reward for service is the strength to serve.' "

Chapter X

A LEGACY OF EYES

From Hong Kong Tom wrote, "I still have hopes of some further Medico aid to the Tibetans." Tom wanted to help the Tibetan refugees in their sad plight, particularly since they were such innocent victims who had never waged war in their entire history. He appealed to his friend, Travis Fletcher, who told him it was up to the government of India to give permission to Medico to come in through their country with medical aid. The Tibetans desperately needed help. Tom had seen a mobile van that he felt could be part of the health unit he envisioned for Tibetan aid. He had sent me a picture of the van many months ago. This was an unfinished task at the moment, as well as an unfulfilled promise. The New York City Chapter has been able to send discarded school uniforms to the Tibetan refugees, as well as Dooley kits. Mr. K. S. Gupta of the Central Relief Committee has been a real help in getting our shipments to the Tibetans.

After Tom's visit to the States, his mail became a bigger problem than ever as there was so much more of it. We had to make arrangements to handle it as quickly as possible. Kay Kelly, who had been working on it up to this time, needed help and we were happy when Maureen Brady came on the scene. Her job was to open, read, mark, sort, and distribute the mail for prompt replies. We found out at this time that the *Reader's Digest* was published in braille and, as a result, we were receiving letters and gifts for Tom from blind people. Some requested autographed books and pictures. One of our volunteers, Carol Cantwell, had studied Braille and she was able to answer these letters. When we told Tom about answering his mail in braille, he was delighted.

Harlan Hobbs, Arthur Godfrey and Louise Gore were appointed to a subcommittee to expand Medico's board of directors. Malcolm, acting as the Executive Director, started to lose weight. The minutes of the Board meetings were to be mailed to Tom, which Mal felt was a step in the right direction. To me it seemed strange that Tom had never received them prior to this.

The Disc Team was now busier than ever, and my right arm, Audrey Byrne, helped us enormously. At Malcolm's request, we kept a record of our efforts and at times this was a nuisance. We kept a count of the letters we answered, to see what our efforts were worth in terms of the money Medico saved. We kept a count of the hours, multiplied it by an average salary, and came up with estimated savings of over twelve thousand dollars, which pleased Tom tremendously.

All sort of letters and requests were sent to Tom. We were privileged to meet many wonderful people like Mariette S. Brown, of Montreux, Switzerland, who not only contributed large sums through her husband's Foundation, but would send us darling handmade baby clothes. We were so pleased to be able to send these lovely items to

Tom for "his kingdom full of kids." He was so captivated by some of these letters that he planned to collect
them for a book one day. I was always putting aside letters
he had marked "Special." One lady in Santa Ana, California, was compiling a book of recipes contributed by
gourmets and famous personalities. Would Tom submit
his favorite receipe with a paragraph concerning himself? I
was inclined to write and say his favorite dish was a
Nedick's frankfurter, but I turned this one over to his
mother.

By August 7th Tom was "back in the Valley I have
learned to love so much." On arriving in Laos he found
Ban Houei Sai the same except for a new building three-
quarters finished. He was "beset with difficulties upon
arriving out here, mostly with the Cambodian program. So
far, the Viet Nam team seems superb." Tom resignedly
added, "These problems are the kinds of things I was
absolutely expecting, so I don't suppose I should sweat
much." And Tom went on, "It is amusing, however, that I
leave from one set of administration problems in New
York and find another set of problems here in Asia. I
suppose that is why I appreciate the sunshine and the
daylight so much. It seems that in Medico there is so much
darkness and rain."

The team at Houei Sai and Muong Sing were a salve to
Tom and they were doing a "fine job." Tom's return
home to his valley was celebrated by a *baci* to which all the
village was invited.

Dr. Hughes, a woman doctor, was now at Ban Houei Sai,
and there were two doctors, Dr. Voulgaropoulos and Dr.
Rosenbloom, in Cambodia. Tom had every one "on post"
even if it was not the post originally planned. He loved

being back in his jungle village, and he looked forward to his brother's visit with Paul and Bob Copenhaver in November. Tom had a new pilot, Ted Werner, who helped him greatly during this sad final year.

Realizing the need Tom had for his plane and being aware of the plane's great expense, we set about to farm out projects so its upkeep wouldn't be too much of a financial burden on Medico's funds. It was a comfort knowing that Tom could get his team out quickly should they need to evacuate the hospital, and he had a means of getting to a hospital himself, if his illness made it necessary. One new propeller was furnished by Pius X High School in Lincoln, Nebraska. In some cases we asked for funds for the purchase of gasoline.

By August Malcolm was making a real attempt to run Medico, but despite Tom's request that Malcolm be given authority, it was limited and restricted. Tom's mail often contained instructions for Malcolm that had to be taken off the discs. By the time they were assembled and delivered to Malcolm in a large brown envelope, it was bulging with requests and instructions. Malcolm soon had a name for this brown envelope that appeared on his desk. He called it the "brown bomb." And it was always on his desk early in the morning, as I would leave it there on my way downtown to my own office. It would sometimes take days before every item in the envelope could be taken care of. If you had a busy day to begin with, the "brown bomb" didn't ease the situation any.

Every day the mail brought up some different and unusual offer of help. I recall the offer of a trampoline, which Tom wanted for his hospital compound for the kids. The cost of shipment was too great, however, and we had to turn down the offer. The offer was then translated into dollars and cents, and we received almost $700. On another occasion a real clown, Happy Kellems, of Cleveland, Ohio, was interested in developing Tom's playground in Laos and offered his help.

In the summer of 1960 I decided to take a week's vacation and Audrey agreed to take all the work off the discs when it came in, and Kay Kelly agreed to sign the letters and send them out while I was away. By this time we had about 21 girls on the Disc Team. Kay's pinch-hitting job on the discs amused Audrey very much, because Kay would get so wrapped up with a comment or decision that Tom was making on the discs that she would forget herself and stand up and shout "Bravo!" And if there was anything she didn't approve, she would rise to her feet in objection, ear-plugs and all, pulling the machine with her.

There were times when, despite all the problems, we felt a real sense of satisfaction. One morning, coming to work on the subway, I read that Senator Kefauver was irked at the possible destruction of the unused Salk vaccine. He felt it could be used by underdeveloped countries and not destroyed, since it was good vaccine. I got off the train and left the clip on Tom Regan's desk at Medico's headquarters, since Tom was in charge of drug shipments, and continued on downtown to my job. That day Dr. McAlvie wired Medico asking for Salk vaccine as he had a wire from Jordan that an epidemic of polio had broken out. Tom Regan thought I was psychic, because he knew exactly where to locate the necessary vaccine; the clipping contained all the information he needed.

While Laos was in a turmoil, the provinces were not

aware of the revolution. All the trouble was in Vientiane, and elsewhere things seemed quiet and tranquil. Tom was puzzled so he took off for Bangkok en route to Saigon to find out what was going on in "his" own country. Five or six hundred Americans had already been evacuated from the capital, but some Americans in provincial posts remained. So Tom felt safe to leave the teams in their places. He had to get the team installed at Quang Ngai in central Viet Nam, and he intended to visit with Madame Ngai en route. It was now time to get the 1,000 hour check-up on the plane and Tom had to send it to Formosa. This meant he had to resort to a commercial plane and all the delays that accompanied it. Tom had to fly into Vientiane to make arrangements for many things for the hospital with the "government here, the counter-revolutionary, and the revolutionary which had been united."

Tom had sent Chai down to get things out of the warehouse and, upon his arrival, Chai got caught in the revolution. Chai, however, got the government to give him a DC-3 and he had accomplished his mission and was en route back to the hospital to be on hand for the birth of his new baby. Tom was bursting at the seams with pride in Chai and how he managed his assignment.

Tom told us in September that he planned to visit with his friend, Travis Fletcher, "who will help me work out the program with the Tibetan team." We had some wonderful movie film of Tom and he had promised to do a sound track for us. So around this time we asked him to make the tape for the film. Nothing ever seemed to be a burden to him, but we noticed that he began to talk in commas and periods, due to all the dictation he was putting on the discs!

It took anywhere from seven to eleven days for mail to reach Tom. His reaction to the copy of Cardinal Newman's prayer finally reached me: "Oh, Teresa, how beautiful are the words of Cardinal Newman that you quoted. I must keep them in my notes." You could be sure it was something very special if you found it among Tom's "notes."

Tom's spirits were lifting. On September 3d he excitedly wrote: "Hey, you know I'm going to be home with all of you in about a month from now . . . a little more than a month. Isn't that wonderful! Good Lord, Teresa, prepare for some more hectic days. I can see it now, meet me at the airport, take me here, rush me there, meet me for breakfast, meet me for dinner, meet me at midnight, have you got your pad. Teresa get into a taxicab, Kay Kelly be quiet, I want to dictate something etc. etc. Anyway, I won't be going anywhere except St. Louis and New York, and I won't be talking, so there won't be much traveling around and I'm definitely going to be around that office a good deal so that no one sort of buffaloes me around, and I don't mean Malcolm, *you* know who I mean."

When Tom returned to Laos, he found the plane still in Bangkok waiting departure for Formosa, and the delay was due to a missing overseas radio. Tom had hoped to deliver the mail and all the food which had gathered at the Embassy. With all his duties at the diplomatic level, Tom would have preferred to stay on the job as a doctor—"the root of the tree of me." But there were always other administrative jobs interfering with his one love. Writing to Paul Hellmuth, Tom said, "Oh, Paul, how true it is that technical skill means so little. Human personality—the fibre and core of the individual—this is what counts in our work out here."

Tom's new team was now working at Quang Ngai. "Carl (Dr. Wiedermann) is a superb fellow. How I wish I could keep him in Laos. I am sure he will do a good job." Tom was also impressed with the young African doctor, Mungai Njoroge, and envisioned him as the "spearhead" of all Medico's activities in Africa. Tom wanted a hospital in the Congo, Tanganyika, and in South Africa, as well as Guinea. He saw in Mungai a man who could establish these programs. Tom hoped to see the day when a Chinese doctor would care for an Ethiopian and an Ethiopian an Asian. The horizon for Tom was unlimited.

Paul and Malcolm's pending trip to Asia was postponed to October, and it now looked as though it might be November before they would leave. Tom got to thinking about his new book. He had picked out a title, "The Night of the Same Day." In a note he explained: "You know how I hate to go to bed the night of the same day that I am living, that is to say, I think it's a waste of whatever short length of time I have left on this earth to sleep before midnight." Many a disc ended with the hissing of the kerosene lamp as it ran out of fuel long past midnight.

Around this time, September 1960, we transcribed Tom's comments about Dr. Verne Chaney, at that time in Southeast Asia for three months as a volunteer Surgical Consultant to Tom. Dr. Chaney was later to organize and head The Thomas A. Dooley Foundation. Said Tom of Dr. Chaney, "Verne Chaney was with me in Viet Nam, and today he and Carl are flying up to Quang Ngai in the Apache for a second look to show it to Verne Chaney. He certainly is a fine surgeon and I certainly hope that Medico is able to utilize his help and services again later." If only Tom had known then how much of himself Dr. Verne Chaney was to give to the continuation of his work after Tom's death.

Tom vowed that he wasn't going to stand by and "let things happen" and he had several ideas to propose to the Board, and he wanted time to discuss new business. He was well aware of a concentration of power on the Board. Many of his friends were well aware of it. He planned to suggest that a committee be appointed to study the possibility of Medico being split 1) a group that would run the village-type hospital with the personal touch being maintained 2) a group that would handle research, larger programs, on a less personal basis. He was looking forward to the October board meeting with mixed emotions.

At this point Tom found time to write what was later called his "Dear Bart" letter. It was a man-to-man letter of advice to a young intern, and was intended to be a chapter in the book Tom never finished. Mrs. Dooley reprinted it as the final section of her book, *Promises to Keep.* Tom never felt himself to be a good writer, though many others believe he was. This letter found its way into a recent anthology, entitled *Enduring Prose,* which includes such great writers as Abraham Lincoln and Winston Churchill. It also includes a piece of writing that has inspired many young people, President Kennedy's inauguration speech. It makes me proud to know that Tom's letter is surrounded by such distinguished company, but Tom himself would never have believed it.

In a letter written at 2:45 A.M. on October third, Tom wrote that he was beginning to feel he would never be "productive again as long as I live," if all he did was write thank you notes. His mail was a great concern to him, and he estimated if he were to write 100 letters a day until "the day I die," he would "never begin to thank enough people." There is the story of a blind Chinese girl named Aurora Lee, who taught school in Bangkok. Aurora read the braille copy of *Deliver Us From Evil,* and sent Tom a contribution from her meager salary. When Tom got to Bangkok, he searched out Aurora Lee personally. She served him pineapple on this visit. Some months later when Miss Genevieve Caufield held a luncheon for him, she invited Miss Lee. Much to Miss Caufield's and Miss Lee's amazement, he mentioned the pineapple.

At the Vietnamese Students Convention in the U.S. years later, Miss Caufield told me of a conversation she had had with Dr. Dooley in Bangkok. Tom told her that he hoped to live 60 years. These years would be divided into three parts—the first twenty would be devoted to the education of Dooley; the second twenty to his work; and the last twenty he hoped to devote to Dooley's leisure. Miss Caufield told him he would never devote the last twenty years of his life to Dooley.

Every time there was a government change or revolution in Laos, it created more problems for Tom. Getting shot wasn't the real problem as much as being able to get around. To go from "rebel" land to "government" land, even though the chiefs in both of these areas were personal friends of Tom's, a passport of sorts was needed. With eight tons of equipment tied up across the river in Thailand, where the country would not export to Laos, Tom had to search out a few elephants. But he also had to learn whether the keeper of the elephants was friendly to Captain Kong Lee, or to General Phoumi Nosavan. So often his problems were very strange ones.

On October 6th, Kay, Malcolm and his wife, Gay, and I rode out to the airport to meet Tom. His flight from London was delayed; the arrival time was set for 5:09 A.M. the next morning. It didn't take us long to make up our minds. We headed back for New York, Gay and Malcolm went to Tom's apartment, and Kay and I retired to the Gramercy Park Hotel, putting in a call to be wakened at 4 A.M. We then phoned Gay and Malcolm and all of us drove out to the airport in the dark. We watched Tom's plane land and stood on the "deck" waiting for him to appear. Tom's expression at seeing us lined up at that hour was one of shock and pleasure. He just stopped, put down his luggage, and stared at the four of us in utter disbelief. Going through Customs, Tom made all sorts of gesticulations conveying messages to Malcolm through the glass partition. Before long we were motoring to the city. It was now dawn, the city was quiet, and his apartment looked beautiful as the sun rose and lighted the city. Tom quickly unpacked his bags and, as always, had a little gift for all present. He presented me with a scroll from the walls of an ancient Buddhist Temple, explaining that these were to the Buddhist what a station of the cross was to a Catholic. With each scroll Tom had a little piece of a brown paper with an interpretation of the scroll written on it.

Gay Dooley cooked him a hearty breakfast, and he was obviously happy to be among his books, his art treasures, and home. New York was very much a home to Tom, and though St. Louis held a special place for him, I think New

York outranked it. Tom had lunch with us later that day at the Gramercy Park Hotel, and told us of problems he had getting medicaments shipped into Laos. Then he inquired if I "got on" with one of the secretaries in the Medico office, and I told him that to my knowledge everything was O.K. He didn't say why he asked.

It seemed to me that Tom had some of the nicest friends in the world. A day or two after his homecoming I met Charles and Alice Carroll, and Kevin and Lorraine Brennan. Kay and myself were included in a dinner invitation, and one of the highlights of the evening was a meeting between Tom and the film producer, Marty Manulis. After a few pleasantries the talk switched to the movie about Tom, and Mr. Manulis said it would be in color, it would be humorous, it would be shot in Thailand, and it would be ready in 1962! Much later the film was "shelved," and one day a librarian at 20th Century-Fox wrote to tell me they had an album of pictures with my name on it. Would I like it back? For the life of me I couldn't remember such an album, and I had never had time to make up a scrapbook or album. However, I advised them to return it to me. Its red binder was unfamiliar but there was my name on it, in Tom's handwriting, so I turned it over to Malcolm.

The next day Tom kept an appointment with Dr. McNeer. Mrs. Dooley in the meantime flew into New York and stayed at the apartment. Tom had a surprise in store for his mother and all of us. Around the corner from the apartment was a tiny restaurant that boasted excellent cuisine and a baby-grand piano as well. His mother, Ann Walsh Weiler and I were seated at a table waiting for Tom, when we heard music and saw Tom at the piano. It was the first time he had played since his operation. He played Rachmaninoff, Chopin, the Warsaw Concerto, and songs from *Gigi*. One of his favorites was "To Each His Own." We were pleased and thrilled to see his arm restored, and he looked so good and had such energy that I felt he must have overcome the cancer. When the regular musicians appeared, Tom got up and all the diners gave him a tremendous hand, although I doubt they knew who he was. To me it was a beautiful evening of hope.

The next evening Audrey and I were still working at the office when Tom came back at about 9:30 P.M. He was wrestling with the big problem of the Medico board meeting to be held the next day, October 14th. Audrey left around ten and Tom and I worked another hour or so, preparing for his presentation to the board. We walked up to 53rd Street and discussed the pros and cons of his becoming the president of Medico and staying in New York to run it. Tom felt it would be a great sacrifice to give up being a doctor in Asia to run the head office, and it bothered him. He suggested we stop in a drugstore, and he ordered a chocolate soda as he continued to weigh the problem. Would the office and the program be more efficiently run if Tom remained in New York? Would he do a better job for the program by working overseas, where his heart was?

The board meeting next day was very upsetting to me, as I was greatly concerned over the decisions that would be made. I met Tom when the meeting was over at his apartment; his mother and some of the board members and friends were on hand. On the surface there was an atmosphere of victory and joy, and I was pleased to know that Tom was satisfied with the results. Malcolm did not feel there was any cause to celebrate, however. Tom had been given the position of vice chairman, Bill Patty had been elected to the position of chairman of the executive committee, and Dr. Berman was made president. Tom didn't attempt to "butter up" the board, much to the dismay of Dr. Berman, and in laying his cards on the table he stepped on a few toes. He told the board that he was not interested in persons, only in getting medicine for the sick. In calling a spade a spade, he neglected to use diplomacy and instead substituted a blunt frankness that alienated some of the board. But Tom wrestled the problem to the ground and decided—rightly, I believe—that he was not going to stay in New York.

The next day I drove Mrs. Dooley out to visit with her grandchildren as it was Maureen's birthday. On the drive back to New York she told me she was going to enter the hospital after Tom left, as she was not feeling well. She, too, was concerned over Medico's future and Tom's health.

While Tom was in New York he made arrangements to visit with Hoang Van Ngoan who was attending the Scarborough Country Day School. (Since Tom's death there have been many Dooley Scholarships offered in universities such as Notre Dame and St. Mary's College for Women.) Ngoan was staying with the Northshield family, who provided him with a warm, loving and wonderful home. He had a motor scooter to take him back and forth to school, and his fellow students were eager to be his friends. A few years later, when Ngoan graduated from this school, he was given a tremendous ovation by his classmates and their parents when he stood up to receive his diploma. I was very proud of Ngoan as I sat in the audience, and I felt that Tom would have bounced up and cheered long and loudly, for Tom felt like a father to Ngoan. Ngoan has written us from Chicago about his job during the summer of 1965 as an obstetrical technician: "I scrub, and help doctors deliver babies. The doctors are very kind to me, and they are glad to answer any questions I might have. I actually delivered a baby girl—how about that! The doctor let me do it all, and just stepped aside and watched me carefully as I brought the infant into the world. Because I assisted the late Dr. Dooley in Laos, I was not scared at all. Anyway, I like my summer job and I have been accepted by the School of Nursing." Ngoan likes to play soccer if he has the time to give the game, but most of his time is spent in study. In the summer of 1964 Ngoan paid a visit to Dr. Dooley's grave in St. Louis, and he has remained a dear friend to the man who believed in his ability. It is my fondest dream, as it was Tom's, that Ngoan will go on to big things in his own country.

To our delight Tom decided to take a day off from work and just relax. It was Sunday, October 23rd, and Tom raced about the U.N. excitedly, showing Valounna, a Lao boy, the meeting-rooms of the U.N. and telling him how underdeveloped nations had a chance for survival as long as the U.N. was in action. We took photographs and these turned out to be the last pictures we had taken with Tom. Strangely enough, the U.N. building is in the background. Tom's idea of a "walk" in New York never coincided with mine. As a rule, he would run ahead and grab Kay's hand and tug her along with him. The rest of us would bring up the rear. On other occasions a walk would develop into a few miles that had all the aspects of a hike, especially if you had a brief-case with you.

A few days later I waited for Tom in the garage entrance

of the Waldorf Astoria. My steno book was tucked in my bag and my pencils were sharpened. The meeting of the executive committee was over, and it was easy to tell that Tom was upset. Dr. Pollack, a member of the committee, was invited by Tom to join us so we could drop him off. We rode Dr. Pollack uptown and then veered off for the airport as Tom was flying to Washington. He was very solemn and dug into his attaché case and handed me the used galley proofs of his last book, *The Night They Burned the Mountain,* saying "it might be of some historical value" someday. I took the proofs to put in a safe place. Tom and I discussed the problems that threw Medico into such a turmoil. Tom had suggested that Medico be split, and a committee be set up to investigate the possibility of having two branches. One would be involved with setting up village-type hospitals such as Tom was operating, and the other branch would set up interim programs and do research. Tom told me that some committee members were aghast at the proposed split, which Tom now felt was necessary. From what I could gather, the meeting must have been a hectic one.

In Washington Tom was planning to spend the evening with Prince Souphan of the Lao Embassy, and then he had promised to sit for the painting that Mrs. Kormendy was doing. Bright and early, 7 A.M. to be exact, Tom rang Mrs. Kormendy's doorbell to pose for the last time for his second portrait. These two portraits and a sketch are the only existing portraits that Tom posed for, and Mrs. Kormendy asked me to find out from Tom shortly before he died what he would like done with this portrait. Shortly before he died, I mustered up courage to ask him what he would like done with the painting Mrs. Kormendy was

Betty Moul with Lao Children at Ban Houei Sai.

Margaret Alberding, R.N., with Lao student nurses, Khong Island.

The mobile health unit at work in northern India.

The *Peggy E. Lee* leaving the U.S. for Laos.

Dr. Verne Chaney and Bob Considine with Marlene Thompson at benefit dinner.

Marlene Thompson, on leave from Pan American, at Tibetan refugee school.

The first benefit party of the New York City Chapter.

Peggy Lee (holding dog, gift of Tibetan people) with Frank Schait and the Dalai Lama's brother.

Peter Purdy at the Tibetan handicraft training center.

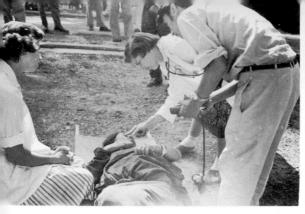

Dr. Virginia Singleton and Vernell Geistweidt, R.N., in northern India.

The Foundation's health unit at work with a native doctor.

Dr. David Stanley, Khong Island, Laos.

Dr. Theodore Reich and Zola Watson, R.N., at Nepal.

Above: Jean Ennis, R.N.,
first member of the Dooley
Youth League to become
a nurse.

Dr. José Castallanos
at Ban Houei Sai.

Right: Dr. Richard
Baldwin, Ban Houei Sai,
Laos.

Delores Frank, United Air Lines stewardess,
instructs Lao student nurses.

Dr. James Dinneen of Portland, Oregon, and family
before departure for Laos.

holding in Washington. He replied, "If the Peace Corps has a building one day, I'd like to see it in that building; if not, with some other organization similar to it." This painting of Tom surrounded by Asian children now hangs in The Thomas A. Dooley Foundation office in San Francisco. The other painting of Tom now hangs in the Dooley Room at Notre Dame.

Tom was sixteen when he became acquainted with Elizabeth Kormendy and her husband, Eugene, who was a professor at Notre Dame. As a student, Tom would often tease Mrs. Kormendy and ask her when she would do a portrait of him. Her answer was always the same, "When you are a celebrity," and as Mrs. Kormendy put it, "He was long a celebrity before the portraits were realized." On this occasion Tom had a last heart-to-heart talk with his "second mother," a title Mrs. Kormendy cherishes since she knew how much he loved his own mother. Mrs. Kormendy made an attempt to serve him breakfast, one that she knew was his favorite, but he ate nothing and, though he joked, he spoke about the shaky condition of his health. When Mrs. Kormendy noticed the conversation turning somber, she wisely suggested he visit Dumbarton College where she taught art. He agreed so Mrs. Kormendy told him to call the college. Sitting on Mrs. Kormendy's couch, he reached for the phone nearby and asked for the head of the Art Department and announced, "I am Dr. Tom Dooley. I just posed for my portrait by Mrs. Kormendy. She has in one hand her palette and in the other hand a very wet brush which she points threateningly toward me asking me, 'Will you visit the college or not?' I will be happy to visit it and can be there in fifteen minutes." In fifteen minutes the stunned Sister Trinita gathered all the students, the teaching staff, the administration, the office employees, the kitchen help, the outdoor workers, and everybody on the campus. It was a miracle of organization. The auditorium was jammed, and Tom was electrifying. He spoke on the stage for fifty minutes. His audience was enthusiastic and the cheering could only be compared to the kind of rapturous cheering the Beatles arouse.

After the talk, Tom dashed back to Mrs. Kormendy's house, grabbed the picture which was five feet by three and jumped into the car with it. Mrs. Kormendy drove him to the Indian Embassy for his visa; he stopped by to visit with the Afghan Ambassador; and then he hopped aboard the plane for New York. I was on hand when Tom came off the plane with the painting.

Soon he was preparing to leave for Asia again. Some girls were on hand to take his picture, and he posed with his traveling kit in one hand and wore his black coat which had been made in Hong Kong. It was a wonderful picture, and the last one taken in the States. Then Tom suggested we go aboard the plane with him. He wanted us to see how he had managed to get three seats together that would make a bed for him, at tourist rates! So we boarded the plane and inspected it from stem to stern. Then we noticed a little alcove set aside as a lounge and Tom, Gay, and I sat down. Malcolm, the ex-Air Force flyer, took off for the navigator's panel up front. Then Tom did something strange. He spoke to me in Lao for several minutes. Very seriously he carried on a conversation directed to me. It never occurred to me to stop him, or insist on knowing what he said. I felt at the time it was his way of saying thank you, so I didn't press for an explanation. Maybe he was aware that this was a kind of last goodbye. It was a terribly sad moment, and after several years I can recall it vividly and with great poignancy.

Bob Copenhaver, Malcolm, and Paul Hellmuth tried to persuade Tom to change his mind about their November trip to Asia. It had already been postponed twice from September to October, and now it had to be a November departure. Paul couldn't make the trip in November, so he dropped out. That left Bob and Malcolm and they wanted to postpone it until January, but Tom was adamant. He said, "It is November or never." And, as the future unfolded, he was right.

Of all Tom's programs I think one of the most outstanding was the Hong Kong Eye Transplant. The starting date was scheduled for January 1961. The problems to be resolved were many, including (1) a permit for an American to do surgery; (2) refrigeration; (3) parents' approval to operate on children; (4) an operating room standing by for emergency use. These things and the cost, Tom felt, were of little consequence. "What IS important is that children in Asia see again." Tom knew the importance of not offending the local Hong Kong doctor by bringing in an American doctor. But if an American doctor could assist the Chinese doctor, this would be different as no one would be offended and no "face" would be lost. Arrangements had to be worked out with the British Crown Colony and Dr. Mattis. Ten days' hospitalization for fifty children had to be provided for; their blindness was caused by vitamin deficiency in infancy and childhood or blindness from corneal opacity. In the Hong Kong area there were thousands of such children, mainly refugees. The group Tom hoped to work on were from the ages of 5 to

15. Adult corneas could be transplanted within seventy-two hours to children's eyes from an eye-bank in the States. The St. Louis eye-bank was to be asked to furnish the corneas, and each cornea was good for two or three grafts. Dr. Mattis planned to take over with him only enough to do fifteen or twenty children the first few days.

It was Tom's plan that the relatives of the deceased would be asked, "Would you like to donate the eyes of your deceased to Dr. Dooley's program? In this way your wife, or husband, will never really die, and his or her eyes will continue to live and through his or her eyes others will see. It sounded to me like a marvelous idea. It was felt that only a few weeks' training would equip the Chinese Ophthalmology Society's doctors to perform this operation with skill. Tom's eyes, which were beautiful and expressive, were to be contributed to this eye bank after his death. The nature of his illness made this wish impossible to fulfill. I had always hoped that some Asian child would be able to look at the horizons that Tom saw, and see them the same way Tom did, with the same love he felt.

In addition to the Hong Kong Eye Program Tom had a new hospital in mind. It was a neat modern hospital in Avicina, Afghanistan, and he felt it would be a "model for all future growth." To be sure that Medico's board was aware of all the work involved in setting up a hospital, Tom set about to make them knowledgeable. He ordered the complete history of the contract and installation compiled and put into a black binder which was sent to each board member. He was so pleased to be able to send American doctors on a rotating basis where "they could be the 'prime initiator' of a better practice of medicine for the whole of the ancient Kingdom of the Hindu Kush,

Afghanistan." Seventy-five days before his death, he dictated a letter to the board about this program from the Kabul Hotel.

In Viet Nam Dr. Carl Wiedermann was anxiously waiting the arrival of Tom and Malcolm. Each hospital had its own special problems. Dr. Wiedermann was a slight man, with youth on his side and a deep sense of dedication. He was an excellent doctor and won many friends in the dangerous area of Quang Ngai, where the hospital had been set up. He was a very sensitive person, and after Tom's death he hopped a plane and flew to New York still in his white uniform in the middle of winter, with no overcoat and a lung infection. He made it a point to stop into the office to talk to me about Tom's death. Pain and sorrow etched the face of Carl Wiedermann, as I told him all that happened. After the evacuation of Ban Houei Sai, a few years later, Carl was killed by a gunshot wound. He was buried in Connecticut, and it was hard for me to believe that I was kneeling at the coffin of a young doctor whose death occurred in a land I had once never heard about. Two fine men had now given their lives for this work.

On November 3, 1960, Senator John F. Kennedy, then the Presidential nominee, proposed the creation of the Peace Corps. He said that many Americans have "marvelled at the selfless example of Dr. Tom Dooley in Laos" just as "many have shuddered at the examples of the Ugly American." President-to-be Kennedy also pointed out that "men who do not even know how to pronounce the name of the Chief of State to whom they are accredited, must match wits with Communist emissaries long trained in the ways and dialects of that nation." Senator Kennedy and his brother, Robert, had discussed the Peace Corps idea with Tom, and as a new idea it had many critics at first. But Tom Dooley wholeheartedly approved the Peace Corps, and I feel that the Corps is a direct result of the work of Dr. Tom Dooley.

One of my earliest motives for helping Dr. Dooley was the thought of what he was giving up. I knew he liked nice things; he appreciated good food; had a tremendous thirst for life, company, and friends; a keen interest in art, culture, and music. The Tom I knew was like any other young man in his desire to have a home, a wife, and children. He felt he was only temporarily putting aside all these things to take care of the program he felt so keenly about. Much of his philosophy came out in the wonderful heart-to-heart talk between him and Danny Kaye. Tom said, "It's not an obstacle to go out and live in an environment different from the environment you've been raised in. Because, if you have five cents worth of adventure in you, that becomes a challenge. In Asia I don't have electricity; I don't have running water; I don't have chocolate-covered peppermints, but I don't especially miss them; and it's a very challenging stimulating kind of thing *not* to have them." This conversation turned to obstacles, such as would arise with an invitation to start up a hospital in the Congo. Danny Kaye said, "The goal that you set up is practically insurmountable in one person's lifetime." To which Tom replied, "Don't you think that anybody who started anything difficult in this world, don't you think the person who started CARE, or who founded the Red Cross, thought that the problem was too big to be accomplished in a single lifetime? But they went right ahead and did it; and the finest thing you can say about these organizations is that they have surpassed the individuals who founded them."

Tom continued, "Today one person can move the world, thanks to modern communications. The power of one person on TV—one popular star with a captured audience is simply staggering. But the power to communicate isn't a gift, it's a matter of sincerity. If we don't believe in what we do, all the play-acting and the make-up, the whole bit, wouldn't count." After a few minutes Danny Kaye asked Tom how he felt about criticism. Said Tom, "Criticism has been flying a bit heavily lately, about Dooley being tyrannical and egotistical, not humble or modest or self-effacing. But it doesn't particularly bother me as long as it doesn't affect Medico. You know that wonderful Chinese proberb, 'Man who lift head above crowd must expect mud in face!' I am a doctor—in my valley I have some forty thousand human beings. Without me and my crew of three assistants and my Lao students, my people would have black magic, necromancy, sorcery, witchcraft, baboon's blood and white cotton strings around their wrists. Without me they have smallpox, diphtheria epidemics, typhoid epidemics, cholera epidemics. Without this little hospital, they have nothing but wretchedness. My satisfaction comes from what I do, not from what someone may say about me. The clinic starts at dawn and lasts until two or three in the afternoon and I, personally, handle maybe 80 of those patients. That's all that really counts."

Chapter XI

GO NOW AND MEET
THY GOD

As I breakfasted on the morning of November 30th, I heard the news that Dr. Dooley was in a Hong Kong hospital. Since Malcolm had not yet returned, I had no way of knowing how serious the trouble was. I did know from various letters overseas that Tom, Malcolm and Bob had spent eighteen hours with Dr. Carl Wiedermann and had left *Carl* utterly exhausted. Tom evidently had taken Malcolm's advice to check into a hospital, after they left. Tom had requested that his notes for his unwritten book, *The Night of the Same Day*, be sent to him in Asia but when I heard he was hospitalized, I postponed sending them.

When Tom's mother heard the news that walking was now a problem for him, her main concern was how Tom would take to a wheelchair. This thought had never occurred to me, and I found myself praying very hard. The idea of Tom in a wheelchair was a terribly frightening one. Mrs. Dooley also canceled the plans for her trip to Asia, realizing that Tom would be returning soon.

Despite his illness, at this time Tom was more than ever concerned over the executive committee and the Board of Medico. To each member he sent a copy of his report on the installation of the program known as Avicina, his latest. To the new Projects Committee Tom sent a four-page letter detailing how the Medico programs were born and implemented. Evidently, Dr. Illiff's "righteous questioning" had prompted Tom to put all the facts down on paper for the sake of the record.

Malcolm finally arrived home on December 5th and went to the apartment to place a call to Hong Kong. He told me that Tom's back was acting up so badly that he found his legs giving out! From the log Tom had mailed to me, I felt the more likely cause might be exhaustion. The log showed such long hours, with no sleep, that I wondered how a person in perfect health could have done it. I fervently hoped his hospitalization was due to exhaustion and that there was no extension of the cancer. I refused to think otherwise and hoped that a few days of rest would solve the problem. I urged Tom to come home earlier, since he planned to be home on the 10th of January anyhow. I used the apartment as a lure, and reminded him how much nicer it would be for him to get home and rest in it than in a hospital. He could work on his book and have a complete check-up by Dr. McNeer.

In the Hong Kong hospital, propped up with sandbags and pillows, Tom now wrote what turned out to be one of his most famous letters. It was addressed to Father Hesburgh of Notre Dame and it was dated December 2, 1960. "Two things prompt this note to you, Father. The first is that whenever my cancer acts up, and it is certainly 'acting up' now, I turn inward a bit. Less do I think of my hospitals around the world, or of 94 doctors, fund-raising

and the like. More do I think of one Divine Doctor, and
my own personal fund of grace. Is it enough? . . . But
when the time comes, like now, then the storm around me
does not matter. Nothing human or earthly can touch me.
A wilder storm of peace gathers in my heart. What seems
unpossessable, I can possess. What seems unfathomable, I
fathom. What is unutterable, I can utter. Because I can
pray. I can communicate. How do people endure anything
on earth if they cannot have God?"

This letter has been engraved in metal and mounted on
a *prie-dieu* at Our Lady's Grotto at Notre Dame University. If Tom had never done another thing, this wonderful
letter would remain as a great memorial and as testimony
that he was a man with all the fears and loves and problems
bequeathed to us as human beings made in God's image
and likeness. The difference between Tom Dooley and
most people is that he was able to put into words what
we all know in our hearts. Tom had the courage and the
gift to write of his feelings and to face up to them. He
was always courageous and, as death approached, he took
it in his stride just as he did life.

Tom wrote other letters from Hong Kong while he
waited for the back brace he so urgently needed from
America. To an old friend he confided: "I'm not good in
an Executive Board meeting. I guess I'm just not the type.
I thought the wise thing to do as Medico grew older was to
get it off the Tom Dooley basis and out of the strong
leadership (tyranny?) of one man. . . . I thought it best
that Medico not simply be the mirror image of Tom
Dooley or that every action that we do have my monogram
stamped upon it.

"I thought, in the past, that with more democratic
action by the boards, advisory committees, sub-commit-

tees, etc. Medico would advance more solidly with the increments now coming to us. But I find that at the end of two years we have not grown whatsoever, except for what I personally have done here in Asia or back in America. With my fancy Board, with my democratic action, with my committees and sub-committees I find only inertia, inaction and internal arguing and bickering. I find no firm leadership in the men whom I have hired."

Tom now checked out of the hospital and into a Hong Kong hotel. A disc finally arrived for me, the first since his hospitalization, and I eagerly tore open the envelope and placed it on the transcribing machine. When my hands were on the keys, all set to go, Tom's voice stopped me: "Teresa, this does not need any typing. It is 11 P.M. on the 6th of December, Wednesday, and I am in a hotel in Hong Kong unable to get to sleep. I received your letter and cards and everything."

He went on to describe his back brace. He said it was now "sitting here on the side of the bed. I give it a pat and say hello. It is a monstrous-looking thing, with a great big metal bar that comes across my pelvis and two up-right bars which come up on each side of my body, and another bar across the front of me on my chest, and a big flat plate that presses on my chest-bone, and another part that presses on my pelvic bone. Then in the back is a great big metal plate, hooked to each side of which is some kind of windlass outfit that you wind up. It screws you tighter and tighter, pushing the top plates back and the back plates forward. What happens is that it completely immobilizes the back. I can't bend, except from the hips on down. By stopping the motion in the back, it lessens the pull on the ligaments surrounding the bone that has decayed, or gotten cysts in it, or holes in it, or metastasis. I wore the thing this afternoon and I feel like I'm in a medieval Iron Maiden. It definitely makes the back better where I have pains, but dammit it gives me pains everywhere else. I know that these new pains will go away as soon as I get accustomed to it, and at least I can ambulate in the thing. Beforehand my legs just didn't work, because the back hurt so much. Anyway, I'm going to give it a try. This may be the sign the Lord is giving me that my time in Asia is up." I burst into tears as I listened.

The brace made it possible for him to get about and purchase much-needed equipment for the hospitals. In this period he actually spent $10,000 on supplies, and made sure that all of them were delivered. He was relieved that the contracts were all signed, and all the arguing over, except for a "little bit" he had to do for the hospital in Cambodia. He felt he could now step out, and "nothing will fall apart, nothing will collapse, and I feel a certain amount of freedom in stepping down."

Tom commented on the mail he received in Hong Kong. "Most of the letters and telegrams have been very beautiful, but one of them was just awful. It was to this effect: 'What the hell, Dooley, why is such an intelligent man like you working himself into a position where he can't do any more good for anybody. Haven't you got any brains, Dooley?' I guess that telegram is not so far from wrong."

In the face of such cruelty and despite the pain of his illness, Tom still had a moment of happiness. He told me in this little chat on the disc that he had a wire from his pilot telling him that Dr. Zalandos had flown to Muong Sing and kept a promise Tom had made to a Lao woman with a hole in her face. Tom had assured her that surgery would be done when Dr. Berman arrived. However, since the plane was not available, Dr. Berman never did reach Muong Sing. Dr. Zlatanos had kept the promise, and Tom felt very grateful. He closed by saying, "Back to bed again for a few more 100 hours. O.K., Teresa, many thanks, bye bye."

The December issue of *Today's Secretary* had just come out with an article on Tom's volunteer secretaries by Barbara Wiest that began as follows: "Have you ever opened a letter to discover a small slip of mimeographed paper reading, 'I am sure you understand what the doctor's mail must be like. He sent this message to you on his battery-run SoundScriber through a group of volunteer typists. Please help Dr. Dooley by accepting this rather strange way of his getting a personal answer to you from his high mountain valley. . . . a half a world away?'" Shortly after this article appeared, my phone rang. The office was empty as we had had a big snowfall the previous evening, and I was the first person on the job. The voice on the phone was that of Gay Pauley, a feature writer for UPI, who had read Barbara Wiest's article. I answered all her questions and the results were fantastic. All of a sudden Tom's secretaries were famous. Miss Pauley's article appeared in forty-nine papers in the U.S. and we had more offers of help.

I have always loved what Bishop Fulton J. Sheen has written of secretaries, and I have always felt that Tertius and I were kindred spirits:

Secretaries endlessly copying briefs and letters must ask themselves: 'What purpose serve I?' For all of these so-called little people in the trivial tasks, it is worthwhile digging out something very interesting that appears in the letters of St. Paul. There is one name that appears only once. We never hear of him again, before or after; he just looks out of the blackness of one moment with a gleam of light, and yet he will be remembered as long as the Scriptures endure. The person was Tertius, who wrote out the letter which St. Paul sent to the Romans: "Paul has just told me that I, Tertius, who have been taking down this epistle from his dictation, may send you my Christian greetings too." . . . The fact is Saint Paul used secretaries, and one of these, namely Tertius, could not resist the temptation to put down his own name at the end of the letter that Paul wrote.

Most of us are links in a big chain, doing obscure work quietly out of sight. To the eternal glory of the little people who do small work, Tertius is recorded as having enjoyed a far greater honor than that which comes to most authors. In the modern world, many secretaries sign their initials at the bottom of a letter. Perhaps someday some one of them, in imitation of Tertius, will write out his or her full name.

What inspired Tertius to do so was the flood of emotions at writing the letter to the Romans; he could not take down those soul-stirring sentences without being a different man. He had to have an outlet for the thrill that was in him. He must speak for himself. He must be a person. Everyone has status when he does his work for God.

A very strange thing was happening as news of Tom's illness spread. People of all faiths were praying for him, and many felt for him as though he were a member of their own family. Having seen him on television, heard him, and having read his books a kinship of great depth had been established. Tom continued to answer his mail in the hospital, and he was happy to tell me that his "portfolio was absolutely empty." His recorded replies to the mail he had received in Hong Kong reached us within ten day.

The Christmas season was upon us, and we had to work fast if we were to get all this mail out in time for Christmas. I mailed the last bundle of transcribed letters on Christmas Eve. As I stuffed them in the mailbox I had a feeling it was the last time I would mail a bundle of Tom's letters. I thought it fitting that the last letters had been typed by Audrey, who had been such a gem of a secretary through the years. The sadness I felt was cushioned by the fact that it was Christmas, and my faith was a bulwark in times of grief.

Tom's hour to say farewell to his beloved Asia arrived. With his friends, the McCarthys, he spent some painful final hours, and still trying to lighten the moment of his departure he joked his way up to the door of the plane in Bangkok. "Pat" McCarthy of La Porte, Indiana, frantically searched for his missing visa and through her tears she saw the inspector wave Tom on the plane ignoring the lack of it, after one look at Tom's condition.

Having been told Tom would be back in New York on the 27th of December, I optimistically hurried to a florist and bought a little Christmas tree and some lights for his apartment.

The 27th was a very snowy day, and we piled into a cab for Kennedy Airport. Malcolm and his wife, and Russ Stewart, the very able publicity man of Medico, and I, were very apprehensive as we headed out of the city.

Halfway there, the cab broke down and we had to climb out into the snow banks. Though the chance of finding another cab was slim, we were lucky enough to stop one that came along within minutes. On arriving at Pan Am, Malcolm checked with the officials and it was agreed that there would be no picture-taking. When Malcolm was told that the pilot had radioed ahead for an ambulance, my heart sank.

As it came time for Tom's plane to land, we were escorted to an area within a short distance of the plane. The blinker lights on top of the police car twisted and turned, casting off their beams, as we watched for the plane's arrival with fearful hearts. We drew up to the side of the ambulance, and I wondered if Tom would have to be carried off. At this point the wheelchair didn't seem as appalling as it had before. How I prayed that Tom would walk off that plane! Somehow it seemed *so* important that he walk off. Suddenly the plane was there before us on the ground. From all over the field, moving shadows took shape, uniformed and mechanized, as the ground crew took positions without direction. The ramp was up and the ambulance doors were opened. Then the plane door opened and Tom was there, standing up, the stewardess beside him. How proud I felt for him! I had so many mixed emotions, I did not know whether to laugh or cry. Tom was asking the stewardess her name, and thanked her as she escorted him to the limousine. He got into the back seat while Malcolm and Gay sat on the jump seats in the back, and I sat with the chauffeur up front. After Tom tried to make himself comfortable by stretching out length-wise on the back seat, he said: "Hello, Teresa, how are you?"

I turned back to answer, and Tom changed his position in an effort to find some comfort. He was very thin and in much pain. I asked the driver to try to speed it up, and when he nodded at the speedometer I saw he was already doing sixty miles, but we seemed to be dawdling along. When Tom finished a few words with Malcolm and Gay, he asked me:

"How much farther do we have to go, Teresa?"

"About ten more minutes, Tom, at this rate."

The driver took a chance and turned into the one-way street that led to the door of Memorial Hospital. Tom got out of the car with his hands in the back pockets of his khaki pants. It was a long walk down the corridor to the last room on the left, and Tom walked it slowly as we all trailed behind. Once inside the room, the doctor in him came to the surface and the nurse was given a list of things to bring to the room: "I'll need a hot water bottle, some bed boards, pillows." And, as if he had waited for the moment for years, he turned on the hot water in the tub asking Malcolm to give him a hand. Gay and I waited for the nurse to come with all the items Tom had ordered.

That night Tom's pain was unmitigated agony. There was no position he could assume that didn't cause some pain either sitting or lying. It was too bad that a doctor was not on hand the moment he arrived, but he made a very quiet entry.

Soon Tom gave me the name of the stewardess who had been so good to him on the plane and he asked that I take down a letter of gratitude so that he could later sign it. It wasn't too long before the doctors arrived and a pulley was erected over Tom's bed which helped him raise himself or turn in bed or reach for something. Tom truly had become a member of the Fellowship of Pain he had so often written about. I had never really seen what pain could do, and I was grateful that Tom was to get some help to relieve it.

The question was still unresolved, was the pain in his spine and the lower part of his back the result of the melanoma, or was it something else? The next day deep radiation and x-rays were administered. Tom ate very little breakfast. The radiation made him feel a little sicker, yet he managed to call me and give me some instructions.

When his mother went to look for Tom's pajamas, she found he always had fresh ones. We finally found out the secret. One nurse in the hospital assumed the responsibility of taking Tom's p.j.'s home and washing them.

They restricted Tom's phone calls and this was a blessed relief. Yet I actually heard one caller say, "You know, Dr. Dooley, my mother is a great admirer of yours. Would you mind calling her and saying hello." This was a doctor making the request—and, sick as he was, Tom obliged!

On New Year's Eve I drove into the city. It was such a bad night that ice covered my car while I was inside the hospital. With all the lights on, the hospital looked cheerful enough, but the thought of all these poor victims of this dreadful disease, particularly Tom, cast a deep gloom over me. I reached Tom's floor, and when I entered his room I found him resting. He pointed to the window sill where there was a white box.

"Happy New Year, Teresa."

"Why, it's a gardenia! Thank you, Tom. How did you ever get such a lovely one?"

I don't remember his answer, and I do remember that with effort I did not cry. I looked out at the lights in the tall New York buildings, thinking of the gaiety that must be taking place on such a night. Then I looked at Tom and listened to the stillness of his room and the contrast made me wonder at God's plan. Tom seemed more at ease, and it was a relief after watching him suffer.

He now wanted to empty out his suitcases, and pointed to the closet. "Teresa, will you get me that big suitcase from the top shelf?" The closet contained his suitcases, typewriter, and SoundScriber. As I struggled to drag his biggest suitcase across the room to the couch, I realized how slowly but surely all Tom's powers were being taken away from him. His strong hands which could lift suitcases, move bookcases, hurl children in the air, operate on broken bodies, express themselves so articulately on the typewriter were no longer the strong hands of a man in good health. Tom struggled with the locks on his bag which previously he opened with quick and certain deftness. It now took the two of us to do it, and I tried to make it appear to be the fault of the lock, but Tom knew better. Once we had the bag opened, he emptied out all the contents on the couch. There were the usual little gifts he brought home as souvenirs, cloth Lao pocketbooks, opium weights, pictures, and autographed bookplates. He seemed exhausted after sorting them out and telling me what disposal to make of them. And that was our New Year's Eve.

Tom's dear friend, Clare Murphy, visited him on January third. Two dear friends of mine, Sisters Mary Joseph and Mary William of the Nursing Sisters of the Sick Poor, phoned to tell me they were praying for Tom.

These were such sad days. Tom's mother found living alone in the New York apartment an ordeal, as she waited in dread of the message she knew she would get on the telephone. Monsignor James Wilders was kind enough to call her almost daily to encourage her.

On January fourth I tore up to the hospital during my lunch hour. If I took a cab both ways, I found I could make it and still have a few minutes to talk with Tom. This time when I arrived, he said: "Tess, I don't know what I'd do without you."

"I don't know what we'd do without you."

"Tess, do you know those slippers you can stick your feet into, made of terry cloth? Do you think you could find me a pair?"

"I know just where to buy them. Saw them today in a store on Madison Ave."

While at the hospital, I always opened Tom's mail and this day there were several thousand dollars worth of stocks for Tom, which had come in during the earlier part of the week. This generous gift cheered him up enormously. Tom's room was filled with flowers and all sorts of gifts sent to the hospital. A nun in the Carmelite Order, after seeing a photograph of Tom drinking out of a Santa Claus mug, sent him a very special mug used by her order and made by the Trappists at Holy Trinity Abbey, Utah. There was a Latin invocation from Our Lady's Litany, and this little brown mug with the two handles was inscribed, "Mother Most Amiable."

Mail often covered the entire couch, and I decided that we just had to have more help if each letter and card was to be acknowledged. We solicited the help of about 20 girls who met as often as possible in a big conference room in my Company. We decided to acknowledge each message personally. It took many months to do so, a mammoth secretarial job, but we felt it was the only way we could truly express Tom's gratitude.

I found the slippers Tom had asked for and he jerked the pulley and sat up on the edge of the bed to try them on. They were a little big, and I was ready to find a smaller pair, but he insisted that these would do. While I was visiting, his lunch came and he ate very little of it. Tom was not eating enough and thought some splits of champagne would put an edge on his appetite, but they did not help.

When the doctor arrived and looked at his chart, he said: "Tom, how do you feel?" "Well, I got by on one dose of codeine today."

That evening on my way to Tom's room for the mail, I met Malcolm and Mrs. Dooley leaving the elevator. After one look at Mrs. Dooley's face, I knew it was sad news. They had just been told that the back problem was related to the melanoma, and that Tom did not have more than six months.

I called Mrs. Dooley the next day, and she said she felt she should take Tom home to St. Louis. She had phoned the family physician there, who said he would come to New York to help her decide. As it turned out, he recommended that Mrs. Dooley return and Tom stay on.

Mrs. Kormendy also came to New York on January 7th. Coming back from the hospital, we talked of Tom's illness and I told her I went to the hospital only when Tom called and asked me to come. She made me promise to go to the hospital whether Tom called or not. Tom usually called me daily but as he got sicker the phone was taken away. That evening Mrs. Dooley joined us and the three of us visited with Tom.

On January 9th, a bleak Monday, I went to pick up the mail. It was about 5:10 P.M. and his door was closed, so I waited. They told me that the chief x-ray man was with Tom. Dr. McNeer came along while I was waiting, and I found myself pleading with Dr. McNeer not to mind the press or the public and do only what he as a doctor thought should be done. I desperately wanted Tom to have a little hope. I stood outside Tom's room praying that Dr. McNeer's message would not be too hard on Tom. I prayed that he would have more courage, and the real import of the word hope suddenly struck me. There were no chairs in the hall, though there was a sitting-room a good many doors away, so I paced up and down, praying very hard. Finally Dr. McNeer came out of Tom's room and I realized I could go in.

When I entered, Tom said: "Tess, it's cancer, just as I suspected. Had to be, with so much pain."

I could not say anything. Now Tom seemed more worried about Medico than about cancer. He said Malcolm and Dr. Voulgaropoulos had spent much time with him discussing Medico's problems. Then he asked:

"Tess, if I die in a month, will you go to work for Malcolm?"

"Tom, you're not going to die in a month. You have to finish your book. I'll help Malcolm all the way. You know I can do more with our volunteers, and this way I can work and not get paid."

"I guess you are right. Don't cancel the lecture tour, the x-ray treatments may hold me."

So he *did* have some hope! Just then Tom's supper tray arrived. As a rule his mother made it a point to be on hand to assist Tom with his meals. This time she was late, so after the tray was in position, Tom said: "Give me a hand, Teresa, will you?"

We got so engrossed in conversation that I forgot what I was doing and Tom had to motion me to get on with the job. I talked of his book, *The Night of the Same Day,* and the notes he had given me: we talked about Carl Wiedermann and the job he was doing; we talked about the office and the programs; and we even talked about dying. And still I did not cry.

The next day, January 10th, the final report on the state of his health was to be made, since the results of all the tests would be in. I could barely face the news myself, and I wondered how Tom could take so much. I asked Malcolm if they would try to spare Tom, but he said Tom insisted on the whole truth. So at 9:10 A.M. that morning Dr. McNeer and Malcolm met in Tom's room and told him that *all* his tests were positive.

The doctors had approved a new brace, which looked rather like a corset to me, but they felt it would give Tom support. When I called him that day and asked him how he felt, he said: "Awful, I can't find my brace. Can you check the manufacturer and call me back?" I called the floor nurse, and she found the brace had arrived and took it to Tom.

The next night, January 11th, I went to Memorial Hospital and found Tom with his brace on. He showed me how it helped him sit up in a chair. It was so good to see him up and out of bed. His brother Ed and his mother had visited with Tom earlier, and he had asked Ed to buy him a bamboo Chinese back-scratcher, which Eddie did. I wondered why he wanted a back-scratcher and I soon found out. It helped him reach things on the table—letters, notes, a book. Tom felt like trying out a more comfortable chair, so I got it ready with some pillows. After he was comfortable he told me, with his eyes closed, the results of his tests.

He got back into bed, and I just sat in silence. Tom then pointed out a few little black spots that appeared on his arm, to show how fast the disease was spreading. He said: "It's no laughing matter, is it? What are you thinking of?"

I said, "I'm just meditating."

"I could be an out-patient and come back for x-ray treatment, or I can decide on chemotherapy."

"Tom, so many letters are advising you to try Krebiotzen. Would it be worth a try?"

"I'm getting the best treatment for cancer right here."

"Well then, maybe you could take the x-ray treatment and come home to the apartment and finish your book. It's only a few blocks."

Tom went on to explain the difference in the treatments, and what the effects might be. "Well," he said, "I'll have to make the decision today."

The couch was full of packages and the mail that had accumulated in little piles. I started to sort it out as Tom watched me. Then he said: "Tuck me in, Tess, and put things in order."

After I did so, and said good night, I left with such a heavy heart that I felt I wanted to die myself.

The next day Arthur Godfrey came to see Tom, and all the Dooley family. Anne Walsh Weiler also visited him that day, and later I arrived with a letter from Dr. Carl Wiedermann, which I knew would be a tonic for Tom's sagging spirits. I read him the letter and gave him a message from Kay Kelly. I left early as he seemed tired, almost too tired to care.

On many of these visits to the hospital, Tom would dictate letters. He had received a letter from Marie McInerney, a teacher at the Robert G. Shaw School for Retarded Children in Massachusetts. For years these children had been interested in his work and had sent him elephants and Lao huts they made from bars of soap. They had faithfully supported his work and I thought their letter would please him. As I suspected, it did. He picked up a pencil and a long yellow pad and wrote a handwritten note to Miss McInerney. The last letter he ever wrote in longhand was a tribute to a teacher and a school with a big heart.

On Saturday, January 14th, while I was shopping I stopped to make a call home and my mother informed me that Malcolm had phoned. When I called the hospital, Malcolm said that Tom had asked me to come in and bring my book. I got there inside an hour, but within those sixty minutes Tom became too sick to work. I went again on Sunday at noon, and stayed with him until 4:30 P.M., reading some mail whenever he felt up to listening. He no longer had the strength to use the pulley.

It was now two days before Tom's 34th birthday. Nettie's Flower Shop of St. Louis had sent him a huge birthday cake with candied flowers on the top. We took it into Tom and he sampled one of the flowers, and asked for a piece of cake "in two hours, or so." A French Lieutenant, Gerald Cauvin, who had served with Tom in "Operation Freedom" in Viet Nam, called when Tom was sleeping and left this note: "My very dear Tom: I thank you for all that you have meant and taught me since the days of Haiphong, and for a deep friendship which is never to cease. I pray for you humbly in your trials."

I had talked to Tom about the possibility of a large bed-rest that could help him sit up in bed. He seemed enthused and anxious to try anything that would help him sit up. So for his birthday the Dr. Dooley Aid Club gave him a white upholstered bed-rest, which Kay and I purchased. It was so big that we found it difficult to transport, but Kay and I managed to get it to the hospital. It was January 17th, his birthday. When we arrived at the hospital we ran into Monsignor James Wilders in the lobby. He explained that he was waiting for the arrival of Cardinal Spellman with Malcolm, saying that Malcolm had already left Medico's office en route to the hospital. Monsignor invited us to wait and meet the Cardinal. Again this was my lunch hour, and I called the office and asked permission to extend my lunch hour.

Soon the Cardinal arrived, and Monsignor Wilders introduced us. Malcolm and the Cardinal walked the long hallway to Tom's room, and Monsignor, Kay and I (and the huge bed-rest) waited outside. As we stood talking in muffled tones, the Cardinal and Malcolm came out. Malcolm told us how Tom had been sleeping and yet, when the Cardinal was announced, he seemed to understand and sat up in bed and clasped his hands in his familiar Asian gesture of prayer and greeting. He listened as Cardinal Spellman spoke. The Cardinal later summarized his talk with Tom: "I tried to assure him that in his 34 years he had done what very few have done in the allotted Scriptural lifetime." As I looked at the Cardinal, I saw tears in his eyes.

Kay waited outside, while I went in to see Tom but he was very sick. I explained the situation to Kay, and she felt it best not to go in. I left the bed-rest and the birthday cake that the Waldorf had baked at the request of Tom's old friend, Arthur Haugh, of San Francisco. But I knew the bed-rest would be of little help and the cake never enjoyed. I found it hard to believe that only three days earlier Tom had dictated thank-you letters to the doctors who helped him in Hong Kong and to Mr. Sam Pryor for his aid in getting the back-brace to him. Tom's room was again full of birthday messages and telegrams, cards, and letters. It took many bags to move all the mail from the room.

Mrs. Dooley in the meantime found her own health declining, and the family physician felt it would be better if she returned to St. Louis, assuring her that if Tom took a turn for the worse she could be back in New York in a few hours. Reluctantly, she agreed. This was January 18th, and she left for St. Louis sometime in the afternoon.

I had been asked to give a talk the next day, and since I was going to speak about Tom's work, I felt I should go home early and prepare for it. I had not visited Tom during my lunch hour, as I knew that his mother and brother would be with him. When I finished at the office at five o'clock, I looked at some letters Tom had dictated and signed. The signatures on two of the letters were so bad that I couldn't bear to mail them that way. I decided to re-type them before I went home that night, and I also felt that these were the last three letters I would ever mail for him. After I finished the letters, I suddenly decided to run up and peek in on Tom and find out if he needed anything.

When I arrived, the male nurse was on the job and the doctor was just leaving Tom's room. I was shocked to find Tom looking so bad. He was propped up in bed, looking very sick. His eyes were closed. One of the many green scapulars that had been sent to him was in my pocket and I took it out and pinned it to the lapel of his pajamas. At the same time I took out a relic of St. Thérèse, the Little Flower, and placed it in his hand. I asked the Little Flower to intercede for Tom, and ask God to take him out of his pain and suffering.

"Tony, how is Tom?" I asked the male nurse.

"His pulse is good, pressure is O.K., and he's aerating O.K."

I walked to the other side of Tom's bed and felt his forehead. As I circled the room, I noticed a little card with a priest's name on it.

"How did this get here, Tony?"

"Father Mullins, from St. Catherine's Rectory across the street, left it in case you needed him."

"Tony, Tom looks awfully sick to me."

"Miss, do you want me to call the doctor?"

"Wasn't he just here?"

"Well, they don't mind coming back."

"But I'm not a member of the family. Would they object if I were to ask the doctor to come back?"

"If you feel you want the doctor, you can send for him."

I decided to kneel down and say the rosary for Tom, and I took out my rosary and knelt down on the left-hand side of the bed, so that I could look at Tom as I prayed. As I started, I could see his fingers begin to move in the motion of the rosary.

When I finished the rosary, I decided to send for the

doctor and I felt it urgent that I try to reach Father Mullins. The doctor arrived in no time at all, and out in the hall I asked him:

"Do you think I should call the priest?"

"What list is he on?"

"What do you mean?"

"Is he on the critical list?"

"I don't know."

The doctor then stepped into the room where the linen was kept, and called to find out about Tom's condition. When he hung up, he said: "He's not on the critical list, and we usually send for the priest only when the patient is on it. But you should do what you think best."

I debated with myself and I decided to call Father Mullins. At the first call, he was finishing Benediction and when I called again, he was out. The next time I called, I asked if any priest could come over to give Extreme Unction to Dr. Dooley.

Just then the nurse came down the hall and said, "While you are at it, you'd better call Mr. Malcolm Dooley in Huntington." I looked at her in shock. This was the first official indication of crisis.

As Tony Stabingas did all he could to keep Tom comfortable, I watched with sadness the ravages of his illness. Before too long, Father F. X. Finegan appeared on the scene. I knelt while he proceeded to administer the sacrament, and I listened to his final words as he bent down and whispered into Tom's ear, "Son, go now and meet thy God." It was an overwhelming thought.

Then he motioned to me to step outside. "Do not talk in the room. Remember, the patient's hearing is the last sense to go."

"I'll walk you to the elevator, Father. It was good of you to come over."

"That won't be necessary, Miss Gallagher, I have to make a stop at the desk anyway."

"Thank you again, Father. Good night."

I walked back into the room, and went up to the head of Tom's bed and stood where Father Finegan had just been. As I looked down at Tom, I marvelled how peaceful he suddenly looked. As I picked up his hand and put my other hand to his forehead, I realized he was no longer breathing.

"Tony, Tony, I think Tom just died."

"Let me see, let me see. You're right."

"God is good," I said as I saw the look of utter peace on Tom's face. It was 9:40 P.M.

In a flash, Tony disappeared from the room and things began to happen. My greatest concern was to notify the family before the news got out to the press.

I tried to get Malcolm again at home but he was still in the city. I called St. Louis and finally located a close friend of Mrs. Dooley's to be with her when she got the news. I cautioned the nurses against giving out the news to anyone until we were sure that Mrs. Dooley had been informed in St. Louis and Malcolm on Long Island. I then phoned Paul Hellmuth. I was on the phone again, when Malcolm's car turned into the driveway of his house in Huntington. After making some phone calls, Malcolm turned right around and came back to the city.

By the time he and I walked into Tom's room again, it had in this short space of time been stripped of every sign that he had been there. His bags and personal effects were piled on several stretcher tables in the hall. At this sight I finally had a good cry. Tom Regan, who had arrived with Malcolm at the hospital, was kind enough to get me a pill of some sort. He also set the wheels in motion for the flight back to St. Louis. After we took Tom's belongings back to the apartment, I left New York at 5 A.M. and cried all the way home.

Chapter XII

THE WOODS ARE LOVELY,
DARK AND DEEP

The love, affection, and respect paid to Tom following the announcement of his death amazed me. I was moved by the words of the Chicago broadcaster, who reported Tom's death to his listeners by saying: "We all lost a relative last night. Dr. Tom Dooley died of cancer."

On Saturday, Kay and I flew to St. Louis for the funeral, and I stayed with Mrs. Dooley at her request. At the funeral parlor, there was a U.S. Navy honor guard that kept watch as more than 8,000 people came to pay their respects. I was astonished to see the number of persons who came in chartered buses.

The honorary pall-bearers were a group of Asian students, who escorted Tom's casket to the Cathedral of St. Louis, where it lay in state. A rare honor was paid to Tom at the Cathedral in that the honor guard there represented all branches of the armed services. Over 4,000 people came to the Cathedral while he lay in state. It was here that the government of Laos presented Mrs. Dooley with a posthumous award to Tom, their country's highest—Grand

Officer of the Order of a Million Elephants and White Parasol. Our own Secretary of State expressed this country's gratitude for the award: "This most gracious act on the part of His Majesty in distinguished recognition of the work of Dr. Dooley, a United States citizen, among the people of Laos, whom he held in high esteem and affection, is deeply appreciated."

The funeral Mass was attended by 2,000 people who filled the Cathedral, and was celebrated by Monsignor Gottwald. There were over 40 priests in the sanctuary, and the pews were crowded with nuns. Monsignor Gottwald's eulogy was a beautiful tribute, contrasting the life that Tom could have had with the one he had chosen, using Robert Frost's poem as a text:

"What was it that motivated Dr. Dooley to have these beautiful words inscribed on a medal and placed around his neck? *The woods are lovely, dark and deep.* The poem from which they are taken tells the story of a man riding down a country lane during a snowstorm; he sits out there in a buggy, listens to the snow as it softly falls upon the earth, and watches the glistening effect of the moon as it spreads across the meadow. *The woods are lovely, dark and deep!* It is a scene that appeals to every human being—the restfulness, the repose, the beauty of this world. It would have been easy for Dr. Dooley, as we all know, to have had an easy way of life, it would have been easy for him to have established a comfortable medical practice in this city of ours, or any city in the nation . . . He could have looked forward to all the comforts of life. The woods are lovely, very lovely, very attractive. Then like a sword cutting through the soul comes a decision . . . The woods are lovely, yes, *but I have promises to keep.*"

The Woods Are Lovely, Dark and Deep

The Cathedral was very quiet, as we all listened intently. Then Monsignor Gottwald continued: "Dr. Dooley did not so much serve people, as serve God through people. And not until we grasp that fact do we see the dedicated soul that was his. The greatest life that ever was, was lived in thirty-three years. Dr. Dooley was thirty-four. It makes no difference how long we live, but what we do with the days allotted to us. You can do that much as a boy or girl of twelve; you can accomplish that much at the age of twenty, at the age of thirty, and you may never accomplish it at the age of one hundred."

From Hawaii came flowers and garlands and lovely messages. One lei from Honolulu was accompanied by a poignant message from a little boy: "Dr. Tom isn't really gone. His song will live in my heart and a fragment of his goal with a piece of his fighting Irish spirit will remain in the heart of every person, no matter what race or creed, on the face of the globe. Your Hawaiian son, I love you, Lee De Vault."

Much has been written of the funeral in St. Louis, but little has been told of what happened in Asia. On January 27th, a group of Americans, Vietnamese and French gathered at An Lac Orphanage to attend a Mass being offered for Tom. Next to Madame Ngai's quarters is the nursery dedicated to Tom in 1960; the nursery wall was draped in black. In front of the altar was a long, low table draped in black on which were set Tom's picture and a beautiful arrangement of flowers. It was flanked on all four sides with large brass candlesticks and white candles. On either side, the orphanage school desks had been arranged for the children, while Tom's older friends settled under a vine-covered arch. As the sun began to set, the children's choir from Père Khué's parish burst forth in solemn chant as they sang the Mass that was celebrated by Father Robert Crawford. Among those present were many of Tom's old friends—the Reverend Dr. and Mrs. Pell, the newly arrived Episcopal minister, Major General and Mrs. John Ruggles, Major and Mrs. Homer Flemming, Dr. and Mrs. Tran Sy Don, Mrs. H. Walther and daughters, Mrs. Dawson, Mrs. Osborne, Major and Mrs. Worth and children, Dr. John S. Moorhead, Colonel David Gravneau, General Ehrgat, Mrs. Robb, Mrs. Dan, Colonel and Mrs. Quang, Mr. and Mrs. L. T. Bready, Père Hien, Dominic Mai Ngoc Hue, Monsignor Chuong, Eloise Robertson and of course Tom's beloved orphans. On January 30, there was also a Solemn High Requiem Mass with Monsignor Joseph Hartnett officiating. At St. Mary's in Vientiane, a little church Tom saw being erected but did not live to see completed, Father Matt Menger, O.M.I., offered Mass for Tom before fifty American and Lao friends, including former Premier Phoumi Sananikone, National Assembly President Tiao Somsanith, U.S. Embassy and UN officials, and Norman Cousins, editor of the *Saturday Review,* who attended the services with his wife and stated that "Determination to keep Dr. Dooley's work continuing is genuine and massive."

Tom's letters and messages took on new meaning after his death. The Disc Team transcribed some of his most memorable messages, and I feel that they deserve a spot in this book. To school children he had this to say:

To be sure, when I was your age we had many problems to grapple with, but nothing to the kind you will have when you are my age. You will have to learn how to handle the

population explosion, interplanetary living, the morality of
nuclear living. You're going to have to handle the inter-
relations of the races in the world. You're going to have to
reaffirm the importance of the family. You're going to have
to know how to advance in grace with man and with God.

Though his message to teen-agers is prophetic and
somber, I have seen them respond to it by individual and
group efforts:

You know, all around the world, and especially out here in
Laos right now, great nations are striving fiercely to prove that
a free society such as we have and enjoy is outmoded. Small
little lands like land-locked Laos, underdeveloped as it is, are
stirring out of their ancient sleep and are poised between
chaos and orderly development. You, who are teen-agers today, are going to have to help these lands to develop with
maturity and with intelligence.

You are going to be the ones to grow up and fulfill destiny.
The challenge is flung to you, even more than to me, or to
my father, or my father's father. The world has shrunken
considerably. Jets may have taken the ravel out of travel, but
their doing so has increased the weight of the problems to be
handled.

Please prepare yourselves now for what you must do in the
future. Education can be like a timebomb. You are assembled
now in the classroom, but the explosion comes at a later date.
Learn the things that you must learn. Reach out beyond the
campus and beyond the continent that you live in. Remember
the power of the intangible, the interior forces of your human
spirit. Understand that there is one rule above all rules, the
moral law of God. Work hard in school, amass the things and

the facts that you must need now, and later in your life, when the challenge is flung to you, stand up high and tall and strong and answer it . . . and answer it well.

While putting this book together, I often came across letters and notes containing quotations from St. Paul applied to Dr. Dooley. Tom's mother received such a letter from Father John P. Walsh, Assistant General of the O.M.I.'s in Rome: "You know yourself better than anyone how completely he gave himself to his work among Christ's poor and suffering in that far-off land. His whole heart was in it, every fiber of his being. To me it seems that it was a sort of compulsion on his part. 'The Charity of Christ urges me on,' that's the way Saint Paul put it. But let me tell you something that you may not realize. Something that possibly has not been said. There are about sixty-five Oblates working in Laos. They knew Tom's work first-hand. They saw him at work. They learned to love and to admire him. His example is a treasure for those Oblates in Laos, not to mention all the others who have heard of him elsewhere. And Tom is one of us. I was present when Father General presented him with his Oblate Missionary Cross, and I could see what it meant to him. It is true that he wanted to do something in his own way as an American, to show what America really means at its best and to help save what might be saved from Communism . . . Tom was a good American because he was a good Catholic, trying to be a saint. Here in the Oblate Fathers' General House we are reading during meals the French translation of *The Night They Burned the Mountain*. I can assure you that it helps us very much to read what Tom wrote, because he wrote very simply and his feelings come through the words and leave their mark."

After his death I found out that Tom had spent much time telling people about the work we all did to help him. This came as a surprise to us, and particularly to me, as I never felt we were that important. I always considered we were a few among the many who were all doing what they could in their own spheres. People I never met wrote me letters to express their gratitude for our helping Tom, so I knew that Tom must have told them about our work.

St. Michael's, a grammar school in Union City, New Jersey, dedicated one issue of their paper, *The Sword*, to Dr. Dooley. The main article was written by a young Maryknoller who was a friend of Tom's. Father Lawrence Murphy wrote: "Thomas Dooley, had both (courage and generosity) in great abundance. He was not a saint, if by a saint you mean someone without any faults. He was cocky, and sometimes stubborn, and often impatient; but he had a great heart and an enormous love. One text in St. Paul, that we both liked, gives us some idea of who Tom Dooley's model was . . . St. Paul wrote, 'Recall the generosity of Jesus Christ Our Lord Who, having all things, made Himself poor for you in order by His poverty to make you rich.' Dr. Dooley gave himself. A doctor can have a good life in America, a comfortable practice and the respect of his fellow citizens. Tom chose to 'leave his country . . . and his father's house,' in order to enrich the lives of people in far lands of the earth where misery and disease live side by side in every village . . . Dr. Dooley is dead and a Chapter of the book of life is ended. But the book itself is not yet finished. It may be that one of you, or several, will add some glorious pages."

The mail we received after Tom's death was almost too painful to read. It was also too beautiful to keep to myself, and this book allows me to share some of it. For example, Mrs. Bryan Edwards, a teacher in Lubbock, Texas, wrote: "Teresa, the really great thing is that Dr. Dooley is living on in the lives of the youth of our town. When junior high school students stop their work for a period of mourning; when high school students ask for financial gifts as a memorial; and when college students stop their busy lives for a dedication of themselves to learn a skill and put it to work for good in the world—because one T.A.D. influenced their thinking—then there is eternal life on this earth!"

My cloistered friend in Chicago, my "rear echelon" in prayer, explained sacrifice to me: "Sacrifice does not merely mean doing without a thing. It means giving, it means a consecration. When we give ourselves to God, it means making ourselves and every part of us, mind, body, work, talents, and life sacred to God. It means giving all, and giving blindly, giving when we cannot understand."

From the campus of St. Mary's College, Notre Dame, Cecilia Chang wrote: "I, myself, am most appreciative of him. If it weren't for him, I wouldn't be here at St. Mary's. God made him such a wonderful great man. I hope not to disappoint him by failing in my studies." And from the McKinley School in Illinois, Miss Mildred Walden wrote: "In all my years of teaching, I have never seen a person walk into a school and win children's hearts in such a short time. They love him and they always will. The bulletin boards around McKinley School and in the gym are just full of articles about Dr. Dooley that the children and teachers brought to school." In 1965, years after the death

of Dr. Dooley, these children are still supporting his work.
Dr. Dooley's favorite newspaperwoman, Ruth Dean,
wrote: "I think I express the feeling of all his friends in
saying that all who were blessed with knowing him, loved
him and felt his loss greatly. He was so warm, so kind, so
courageously strong in a world that veers dangerously close
to cold corporate disinterest, mediocrity and tepidity. His
candle really lit the darkness for the rest of us . . . I am
grateful to God that I knew him, even if for only a little
while. I am offering my prayers for the repose of his soul,
but I can't help but believe that Tom already is among
God's saints, for his life here was so much like theirs. He
asked for so little; he gave so much."

Three teenagers stand out in my memory, girls who have
remained constant throughout the years, like Kathy
Schuster of Pittsburgh, Pa. who to this day sends us books
of five-cents stamps to help defray the cost of mail. When
Tom died, Kathy wrote: "I know how you must feel,
because I feel like my brother just died." We prevailed
upon Kathy to test her wings on fund-raising, and she
borrowed one of Tom's records and held a meeting with
some friends. The result of their efforts was a successful
cake sale, but when she wrote I could detect a sense of
disappointment, as if her efforts were not enough. On my
table there were a few acorns that my mother and I had
picked up in the Poconos, and I sent one along with my
thanks for the money the Foundation gained as a result of
her cake sale. She wrote to tell me, "I got the acorn
message."

Elise Sereni, who sent boxes of food overseas to Tom
and his team while she was in high school, won a scholar-
ship to a college in Philadelphia. Elise plans to help

continue Dr. Dooley's work after she gets out of college. Jeanne Ennis, who was so anxious to set up a youth organization while she was a student in high school, is now a graduate nurse and a good candidate for the Peace Corps. As Dr. C. W. Mayo of Rochester put it: "Tom left an imprint on everybody he met. He actually left a part of himself with many thousands of people. He had a spirit which does not die."

One of Tom's closest friends, to whom I sent a detailed letter about his funeral, was Sister Madeleva, and she replied: "What a blessed way God chose to take him home! There could hardly be a more eloquent sequel to his 34 years of life, the last and best of them given to go in his suffering members." I also prize this letter from a non-Catholic: "I have read all of Dr. Dooley's books, and my husband and I have spoken of him and prayed for him almost daily these past months. It was a physical blow to see his face above the story of his passing. Since his television appearances, he had become a personal friend. We are Methodists and I do not know all the processes of your religion (neither does my Catholic neighbor, who also revered Dr. Tom). However, we all feel that someday Dr. Thomas Dooley will be placed on an equal footing with Bernardette and all the other saints—none with better right! And if that day comes in my lifetime, here is one Protestant who will bow down and pray to be more like him. Forgive my writing, but we loved him, and wanted to tell you we share your grief. May God be with you, as He surely is with Dr. Tom."

Occasionally we had a few unexpected responsibilities thrust upon us. A teacher in California found it hard to reconcile Tom's death with a just and good God. She asked, "Why should a man that has so much to offer die? If God is given the credit for miracles, could He not be blamed for accidents and unhappiness also?" I turned to a good friend, a Jesuit, for an answer and he wrote: "Miracles are favors granted by God, not obligations that God has towards His creatures. Actually He owes His creatures nothing, though He is most liberal and merciful and gives to His creatures far beyond their deserts. That He does not do what His creatures demand or think He should do, does not prove Him blameworthy or unjust. The fact is that God does not interfere in the ordinary course of human events. When human events turn to the (at least apparent) disadvantage of the creature, a miracle certainly would be an interference with ordinary human events. When God does work a miracle, it is for some special reason known to Him though unknown to man. In Doctor Dooley's case, we must accept that God knew better than we that a miracle would not be some special advantage, and that the Doctor had earned, and should be given, the reward he had earned. For any of us to wish or want it otherwise truly would be selfishness, wouldn't it?"

Chapter XIII

A KEPT PROMISE: THE
FOUNDATION

Tom used to say in his letters, as he felt his illness catching up with him, "the bird of time is all aflutter, and the bird is on the wing." I was beginning to feel that the bird of time involved Medico as well. In June Mrs. Dooley came to New York and met with Dr. Chaney and Dr. Manny, to discuss how Tom's work could be carried on in a manner he would approve. On the day of Tom's death Dr. Peter Comanduras, then Secretary-General of Medico, had been in Monterey, California, on a speaking engagement. Dr. Verne Chaney, having previously worked with Tom in Southeast Asia, was then in the private practice of thoracic surgery in Monterey and had been so for several years. At that time, Dr. Comanduras had asked Dr. Chaney to take a leave of absence from his very successful practice to serve with Medico as its Field Director in Asia. This Dr. Chaney had agreed to do and joined Medico in February, 1961. Dr. Chaney had had previous experience in this type of work in Labrador and Newfoundland as a medical student, in Korea as a battalion and regimental surgeon, and in Haiti as Chief of Surgery for the Hôpital Albert Schweitzer of Dr. Larry Mellon. Dr. Chaney was now much concerned over the mobile health unit that Tom had promised the Dalai Lama, but the leaders of Medico were not inclined to recognize this promise. A new policy at Medico also indicated that the volunteers who assigned projects were no longer needed. This truly worried me, as it was a real departure from Tom's idea of the person-to-person approach.

On June 28th I learned that two of Medico's valuable employees had been fired, that Dr. Manny had submitted his resignation in protest, and that it had been accepted. I was stunned. The daily subway ride to New York is always an ordeal, but the morning of June 29th was a very black one. I decided that the Disc Team must take a stand and protest the acceptance of Dr. Manny's resignation. Dr. Chaney asked us to continue to do his work, for the time being, and shortly thereafter he too resigned from Medico. I decided to discuss the whole thing with Malcolm before taking any final step. I phoned Malcolm and told him I felt it was time to resign, in the light of recent events. He said he would think it over and call me back. Before the day was out, he called and said, "Go ahead." Audrey and I worked late that evening on a draft of a letter to Dr. Bockus. Except for Tom's death, I cannot recall feeling so bad about anything as that letter of resignation.

I then called Mrs. Dooley and told her of our decision, and read my letter to her. She listened quietly and asked me to read it a second time, which I did. She then approved it. In fact, she wanted to do likewise, or at least come to New York to address the July 9th meeting of Medico's board but Malcolm advised her against it. I often wish she had come, and she was never convinced that she did the right thing by staying away.

I mailed our letter of resignation to Dr. Bockus just before leaving on vacation, and when I checked in at my hotel, his reply was waiting for me. It was a very gracious letter, and he asked the volunteers to reconsider, promising that an executive committee meeting would be held and all the problems given consideration. Mal and Gay had sent some lovely flowers to the hotel, and when I called to thank them they told me the good news that a new Dooley had arrived and she was to be called Teresa.

True to his word, Dr. Bockus called an executive committee meeting on Sunday July 9th, and it lasted all day until 6:30 P.M. It was resolved to hire someone as an experienced administrator, since a reorganization was evidently needed. Some of Tom's close friends on the board hoped they could "save" Medico but Mrs. Dooley said she would have nothing further to do with the present program. It became obvious to Dr. Chaney that the executive committee had little power, and he felt the only way to save Tom's work and to continue it was to set up a separate Foundation quickly.

Mrs. Dooley had given much thought to the idea of a Foundation to continue her son's work, and after weeks of deliberation and many talks with Dr. Chaney, myself and others, she was convinced that the Foundation was the answer. Malcolm wanted to wait thirty days to give the executive committee an opportunity to show good faith, and produce the results they promised. I preferred to wait for Malcolm to decide whether he would act now with his mother and Dr. Chaney, or hold out. I was mindful of my promise to Tom to "work with Malcolm."

On July 24th Malcolm and I, Audrey, Kay Kelly, Dr. Manny and others arrived at Dr. Chaney's apartment. The mobile health unit promised to the Tibetan people had been cancelled by Medico as a promise made by Tom Dooley and not by Medico. We knew it was a case of "now, or never." On Sunday, July 30th, Verne went to St. Louis with the papers that would set up The Thomas A. Dooley Foundation, and Mrs. Dooley signed them. Though Verne had set the wheels in motion, he was still willing to stop them and withdraw the papers, if some sign of unity and agreement or reorganization could be reached. He had worked in Asia where the needs are so compelling that a sense of urgency is impressed on a dedicated man. Verne called me many times and did not have to convince me that I should go along with him and Mrs. Dooley. However, I reminded him of my promise to Tom to help Mal, and I felt it best to wait until Malcolm reached a solution. Dr. Chaney had the support of many of Tom's good friends, who agreed to the need of the Foundation.

On Saturday, August 12th, Malcolm called me and said that no decision had been reached at the meeting of Medico's executive committee. He said he would call Verne after he talked to me, which he did. Then I had a call from Dr. Chaney, who said he was pleased with Malcolm's position. I was puzzled, as I was unaware that Malcolm had made a decision. He explained that Malcolm had decided to serve on both the Medico Board and The Thomas A. Dooley Foundation Board. I called Malcolm to get everything clear in my own mind, and he said this decision came up when he spoke to Dr. Chaney. This paved the way for the volunteers to join in and support the Foundation as charter members.

A Kept Promise: The Foundation

Tom's old friends also rallied to the cause. From as far away as Maine, they rode down to New York on a hot summer night driving all the day to make a meeting at night. Jay and Peter Holt, Ted Werner, Tom's pilot, Dr. Manny, Gay, Malcolm, Wayne McKinney and myself met to figure out a way to get the Foundation on the road and Tom's hospitals in Laos re-opened. Our first goal was Ban Houei Sai, and later we hoped for Muong Sing.

Dr. Chaney asked me to be a member of the Board, and told me the first meeting of the corporate members would be held in California. My European trip went out the window when I purchased a plane ticket to San Francisco. Malcolm and I flew there on September 14, 1961. We had hardly checked into our hotel when we were notified of a meeting that would take place in Mrs. Dooley's suite at the Mark Hopkins. The members of the Corporation were enlarged to include Malcolm, Dr. Wiedermann and myself. The original members were Mrs. Dooley, Dr. Emmanuel Voulgaropoulos, Dr. Verne Chaney, and Dr. William Van Valin. The Foundation set up headquarters in San Francisco because California had been the largest contributing State to Tom's work. Not only did Tom have many good friends there, but Dr. Chaney and Dr. Van Valin had their practice in California. In addition, the Foundation in California would not easily be confused with Medico in New York. At a press conference on September 15, 1961, Mrs. Dooley announced the birth of the Foundation.

I could hardly wait to get back to New York to report to the volunteers who were anxiously waiting to hear the results. The same problem faced the main office in San Francisco and the New York City Chapter: we both needed office space. We also needed a mailing-list and since we could not use Medico's, we did the next best thing. We were given the use of some office space at the Waldorf Astoria after working hours, and we went through all our own records from the piles of papers we had saved. As a starter list, we had over 15,000 names!

The main office found space at 442 Post Street, San Francisco. As a Chapter we were not authorized by our budget to spend money on rent, so we had to find space where we could all work without paying rent. Where could one hope to find such a spot in New York? But miracles do happen. Omnia Properties gave us the "unrentable space" in a penthouse on 220 Fifth Avenue. One room in the penthouse is ours, and we shared the area with the girl elevator-operators. We are even listed in the Directory, thanks to Mr. Matthew Sweeney, manager of the building. We were also given the offer of all the paint we could use, and as I explained in the opening chapter, that was the genesis of the office with a red door.

Tom's death did not deter the friends he made in my Company, who helped him through the Dr. Dooley Aid Club. After I returned to New York, they threw all their support behind the Foundation. Our Mail Division is just one example of the constancy of the support we have received over the years. Every month without fail for the last three years one man, Vincent Gugliotti, comes up to my desk and gives me an envelope with ten dollars collected from his co-workers, plus one dollar he always adds himself in my presence. This money has been a godsend in paying postage bills, and any number of emergency uses that keep popping up.

A Kept Promise: The Foundation

Our major task as a Chapter is fund-raising. Yet we must have volunteers to pick up the mail, receipt money, answer letters, pick up phone messages, and keep our books. Also with every fund-raising task, there are numerous committees. At our first annual benefit at the Waldorf Astoria, we were honored to have Vice President Lyndon Johnson and Lady Bird Johnson stop by on the invitation of Mrs. Dooley, our guest of honor on this occasion.

On December 19th, only four months after the Foundation was born, a dramatic meeting was held in the office of Spyros Skouras in New York. Board members Carl Nichols, Dr. Chaney, Dr. Van Valin, Dr. Voulgaropoulos, Malcolm, Mr. Skouras and I were on hand. Audrey recorded the minutes in Mr. Skouras' plush office. Mr. Skouras first explained how little time he could give us, and the reasons why. But Dr. Chaney went right ahead while Mr. Skouras got out his worry beads, which fascinated me as he clicked away at them. Dr. Chaney's enthusiastic and vivid picture of the work we were trying to do seemed to me to be reaching Mr. Skouras, but nevertheless he told us he had to leave for a 6 P.M. appointment. After he left everybody seemed optimistic, but I was not. When we left his office much later, we bumped into him on our way out. He walked us to the elevator, wished us a Merry Christmas, and the elevator door closed. Before we started our descent, the doors suddenly re-opened on orders given by Mr. Skouras. He said: "We will work together to make this Foundation a hit."

"Hip, hip, hooray" was our simultaneous reply. Down went the elevator as our spirits soared to the sky.

One day I got a call from Malcolm, whose office was up

in the fifties. Dr. Van Valin was in from California and told me he just had word that the Foundation would be invited back into Laos to re-open Tom's hospital at Ban Houei Sai. I was elated. I felt Tom was on the job. When the good news finally appeared in the papers, the world knew that Tom's hospital had been re-opened and that The Thomas A. Dooley Foundation had done it.

At Christmas time, Mrs. Dooley was ill in St. Mary's Hospital, and she felt that once she got over the first Christmas without Tom she would be fine. Over the phone she recited the prayer of St. Francis of Assisi: "Lord, give me the serenity to accept what I cannot change, the strength to change what I can, and the wisdom to know the difference."

On Tom's birthday, January 17, 1962, The Thomas A. Dooley Foundation presented the mobile unit to the Tibetan refugees working through the Central Relief Committee.

The Foundation is now in its third year. Dr. Howard Rusk wrote a marvelous account of our work for the New York *Times* under the heading, "Tom Dooley's Heritage":

On the island of Khong in the Mekong River area of Laos, near the Cambodian border, is a 20-bed hospital staffed by an American physician and a Canadian nurse. The physician, Dr. David Stanley, of Maryville, Tenn., has his wife and two children, two and three years old, with him. In addition to the hospital, which has an active outpatient department, the unit has a river clinic program that takes its medical team to the people on many other islands in the area. Since the area east of the river is occupied by the Pathet Lao, the hospital staff cannot use the road north to the provincial town of Pakse.

This medical outpost, in one of the world's most politically troubled areas, is one of the programs in Asia operated by The Thomas A. Dooley Foundation.

The work of Tom Dooley, known in Laos as Than Mo America, or Dr. America, began in 1956, but it is far more active than it was even at the time of his death. The Foundation's largest program in Laos was started at Ban Houei Sai by Tom Dooley himself, with a team of five persons. A 20-bed hospital here takes care of 50 to 100 outpatients daily. It has two boats which extend north to the Burma border and south as far as security permits, currently, about 30 miles. The patients consist of a large number of refugees from the mountain tribes of northern Laos, the Meo, the Yao, and the Black Thai. There are 25,000 refugees in this area. The Dooley Foundation hospital is their only medical service.

The Foundation's newest program in Laos is a 200-bed civilian-military hospital in Pakse. This is being developed into a medical center for southern Laos, not only for treatment, but also for training physicians, nurses, technicians and midwives. Its $25,000 mobile X-ray unit is the only one in southern Laos. The Laos program is administrated by Albert Harris of New York, a former Navy medical corpsman who was a close associate of Dr. Dooley.

Dr. Verne E. Chaney, of Monterey, California, executive director of the Foundation, hopes to have an airplane soon to use as a flying medical clinic for remote mountain villages not accessible by jeep or boat. The California Junior Chamber of Commerce has pledged to buy the aircraft by the novel means of collecting one book of S & H trading stamps from each member. About 12,000 books each worth $2 in cash would be required. All of the vehicles, boats, jeeps, and trucks of the Foundation are painted bright orange. Regardless of language or dialect in this illiterate land, the color is recognizable. It means: The Dooley Foundation, American doctors and nurses, and hope. Each vehicle is identified with a Disney character whose fantasy and charm reflect some of the warmth and humor of America.

In addition to its program in Laos, the Dooley Foundation assists an orphanage in Vietnam and is planning to send two surgical teams to one of 28 surgical pavilions built by the United States in existing civilian hospitals. Today only four of these units have been staffed, but an international appeal by the United States brought responses from 10 nations, which have agreed to send surgical teams. The nations are Japan, Korea, Australia, New Zealand, Great Britain, Canada, West Germany, Italy, the Philippines and Spain.

The Foundation also operates a mobile medical-surgical van with two smaller jeep-trailer dispensary units in northern India serving some 100,000 Tibetans who have fled Tibet since the Communist aggression and the flight of the Dalai from Lhasa in March 1959. It is also providing a husband-and-wife team of two teachers, Peter and Susan Purdy, to teach Tibetan refugee children in Mussoorie in northern India.

A unique project in Mussoorie began early in 1962. Stewardesses from the Pan American and United Airlines spend two to three months as volunteers working in the Foundation's programs as jeep drivers, teachers or nurse's aides. Pan American provides free transportation. The girls contribute their time and the Foundation pays their expenses.

In Nepal, His Majesty's government has requested the Dooley Foundation's assistance in carrying out a national health survey. The School of Public Health of the University of Hawaii is providing the technical supervision of the survey program which will take three years. In addition, the Nepal

A Kept Promise: The Foundation

Minister of Health has asked the Dooley Foundation to assist in a 50-bed hospital in the Rapti Valley of south-central Nepal. The hospital was built and equipped by the United States Agency for International Development. Nepal hopes to augment the three-member team there now with medical specialists on a short-term rotating basis.

Tom Dooley was a rare human being who found the single thing he wanted to do in life: to make the wretched, hungry, sick and hopeless people of Asia understand the best of America through the mercy of medicine. Tom Dooley continues to live in the hearts of the deprived people of Asia. His life and the continuing program of the Dooley Foundation stand for the best in American traditions.

Chapter XIV

THE HERITAGE OF
DR. TOM DOOLEY

Let youth take courage from the story of a young man of their day who loved all the things they love. Dr. Dick Baldwin, age 25, who was in school when Dr. Dooley worked in Asia, was encouraged by Tom's work to get his medical education. From the hospital in Ban Houei Sai, he tells how the Dooley heritage is alive and working:

"The valley is indeed beautiful. The muddy brown of the river is well contrasted by the deep green of the surrounding mountains. The burning of the mountainsides to prepare for the planting of the opium fields is truly the marvelous sight Dr. Tom describes in his book. Dooley couldn't have picked a better spot. It's truly a marvelous place to work. I am telling you this because most of my friends feel quite sorry for me 'stuck in the wild jungles of Laos.' On the contrary, it is I who am sorry—for them. For their concrete streets and cement buildings are no match for the lush green paradise in which I find myself.

"The pace of living here is slow and deliberate, and sometimes not too much of the latter. It is a real change from the go-like-hell atmosphere of the San Francisco area from which I came. It took some time to slow myself down, and when I finally did, I realized that this was certainly the more enjoyable and rational way to live. The medical needs of these people are overwhelming. For each old man I treat for tuberculosis, there is another to take his place. For each woman with malaria, there are ten more with her. For each child—pot bellied and spindley-legged from malnutrition, there stand a hundred more behind him, each suffering more than the last. We can and are helping the people, but at times our efforts seem so meager. The future of The Dooley Foundation in Laos lies in teaching the Lao to help themselves.

"You ask me if there is anything special I want. To be perfectly honest with you, there is so much difference between myself and the people around me that by comparison I live like a king. Yes, I sure can use those T-shirts; not for me but for the Lao who work for me—many of whom have only one shirt to their name. To be able to see them enjoying some of the things I am able to enjoy—that would be the best gift you could give me. Most of our help here now are the original Lao staff with whom Dr. Dooley worked. It would be hard to find such hard workers back in the States. They sure deserve a lot.

"I, being young and single, unfortunately, have been drafted. I'm due to go into the Air Force on the 9th of November. This puts an abrupt end to my work here with The Dooley Foundation. But I hope it will be only a temporary one. I still have a month and a half here, but even at that it seems so short a time in which to do what I want.

"There are other jobs out here with The Foundation

than that of doctor or nurses. If you are serious about this, it would merit a letter to the home office in San Francisco. They might have a place for you. The monetary gains would be nothing, but there is so much more to life after all, than that."

Margaret Alberding, R.N., of Canada is working on Khong Island, Laos for The Thomas A. Dooley Foundation. Margaret admits to loneliness, but she is compensated in no small way by the esteem and affection of the students. Margaret has a program of nursing care for mothers that is going well, with UNICEF and WHO helping her with items she needs. The nursing program was not to have more than three girls, but Margaret said "some of the girls even cried when they found out that we would not accept more than three students. Then the Lao doctor asked us to take them anyway, and he would assume responsibility for their supervision. Tim Ford, as you may know, has returned to the States with his little adopted Chinese refugee boy. An old building (made from cow dung and mud) which is about 20 years old is at present being repaired for me to hold classes and later on as a maternal health clinic. It is not in the best of condition because Dick (Blanchefield) leaned against the wall, and it promptly fell out. Then the carpenter came over, and he fell through the floor! However, with a little re-enforcing, whitewash, and general decorating, it should be my very own, and I'll make it a palace."

From the island of Khong we also hear from Dr. David Stanley and his wife who are the first American couple (with blond, blue-eyed boys) the Lao people have ever seen. Khong is an island 18 miles around in which the 15,000 or more inhabitants travel mostly by foot. Some have bicycles, fewer have motorcycles, and a very few have jeeps given them by the U.S. Government. Many of the jeeps are often in poor running condition, as parts are difficult to obtain. The plane that brought the jeep to the school inspector provided Dr. Stanley with a new patient— a little boy who fell out of the jeep the day it was delivered and broke his arm.

"Imagine," says Dr. Stanley, "having eight or ten strange people walking in and out of your house, touching your clothes, your hair, your skin. Imagine having three people squatting by your children's bed when you tuck them in at night. Imagine people watching you comb your hair and brush your teeth, and then using your comb and toothbrush themselves! Imagine having 30 or more people flocking around you in town.

"This is what we have every day. The Lao live so very close to each other that within every little village they seem to be one family. Certainly we feel as if we have been adopted too. There have been many times when I have walked into our living-room and found all the chairs full—sometimes with strangers only. It is not unusual for a passerby to stop in for a drink of water. Whenever we ride on the motorcycle, people shout to us in Lao from their doorways, 'Where are you going?' "

Mrs. Stanley said that the people in Laos were delighted when she and her doctor husband spoke to them in Lao. Her two boys, Paul and Dan, have taken to the language like ducks to water and know how to speak it better than their parents. Paul and Dan particularly enjoyed the New Year festival, celebrated there in April. The party goes on for five days and "water throwing" is the favorite sport, much to the fun of all. Everybody soaks everyone else, and this symbolizes the washing away of the old year's sins, disappointments, and the coming of the cool rains which soon follow.

Dr. Stanley described his new home: "The house we live in has mud walls, no electricity, no running water, beds with no springs, charcoal cooking pots, a leaky roof and numerous bugs, frogs, lizards, rats, snakes, chickens, dogs, and people coming in and out. And if this is not enough, a large pig and family live under our kitchen! Try as we may, it is nearly impossible to keep the house clean—at least by American standards. One day Nancy was determined to get the kitchen halfway clean, so she scrubbed the floor with a wire brush. Well, everyone thought she was crazy! They were so amazed to see someone clean up the kitchen that our help ran to bring other people to *watch* her.

"It is so easy to become discouraged when we want to do so much and see how slow progress is made. However, we are finally realizing that we cannot change centuries of habits overnight. We hope to have taught them a few things. Perhaps we will be the last Americans they will see, perhaps they will remember us and things we did together for a long time. Perhaps they will tell their children about us. Perhaps we have taught them a little about how a democratic American Christian family lives."

In August of 1964 Tom's mother was buried next to him in St. Louis. While I was unable to attend her funeral, my spirit and heart were there from the moment I called St. Mary's on the 19th. She died later that day. Prior to her last fatal illness, a young man from Israel who signed his letters "A Guy named Joe," had written to Mrs. Dooley telling her of his esteem for her son. Joe heard about Tom from a former Navy man, now a Baptist minister in Israel who had known Tom when he served in the Navy. Joe informed Mrs. Dooley that he planned to arrive in New York in early August. Mrs. Dooley shared Joe's letter with me, and when he came to New York Betty Moul arranged to meet him and show him some of the sights. Before he left, I phoned Mrs. Dooley to find out if she was well enough to have a visit from Joe Tienfenthal in St. Louis. But she was now too sick to see him and was soon hospitalized. When Joe arrived in St. Louis, Mrs. Dooley was gravely ill. Joe gave Malcolm a small medal for his mother that had been blessed in Jerusalem before he left, and he then visited Tom's grave.

The year 1964 ended with the Foundation having taken several big steps. In New York we gave our first $50 a plate dinner and in San Francisco the first "Splendid American" Award was made. Our New York Chapter is busy making up Dooley kits to be used in our programs overseas. Mrs. Robert Knight and some residents of Leisure Village, Lakewood, N.J. meet weekly to sew pajamas and the cloth kit bags that are to an Asian child what a Christmas stocking is to an American child. To the Asian, however, these items are luxuries.

When Dick Blanchefield returned from a stint in Laos he was concerned over the magnitude of the job and the mountains of medicine that were needed. Many days he worked without anybody to talk to. With no telephone, no newspapers, no radio, he said his only conversation was with God. This ex-Marine found the Laotians wonderful people with a marvelous sense of humor. Medicine is so expensive in Laos that the local doctor has to dole out the vitamins in small amounts to make it go around. It is no wonder that death often strikes early in Laos.

In August 1965 Dr. James Dinneen, an Air Force veteran who served on Guam and Okinawa, and his wife Dorothy, a former teacher at Eliot School in Oregon, left to work at the Foundation's hospital in Pakse, Laos. They have taken their four children with them, ranging in ages from four years to nine months. When Dr. Dooley was on a lecture tour in Portland, Oregon, after his cancer operation, the Dinneens heard him talk and resolved to follow his example. This was prior to their marriage. Now they have sold their home and stored their furniture and auto until their return after eighteen months in Asia. This wonderful American family is a living and inspiring example of the Dooley heritage.

This medical work in Asia and elsewhere today is a small part of the heritage of Dr. Tom Dooley, which goes on and on, and grows and grows, because it is fed by a never-ending source, charity, which is love. The Thomas A. Dooley Foundation stands for all the years of work and suffering and love that Tom contributed. Whenever I hear anyone question the value of Tom's life and work, I remember the story that Dr. Verne Chaney once told us at a meeting after his return from Asia and Africa. He had stopped by to see Dr. Albert Schweitzer at Lambarene, and he had asked the doctor, who was approaching his 90th birthday and running a fine hospital, what he would do if he had to live his life all over. Dr. Schweitzer looked at him and said, "If I had to live my life all over again, I would like to do what Dr. Dooley did."

It was Pope St. Gregory who said, as long ago as the sixth

century, "He that hath a talent, let him see that he hide it not. He that hath abundance, let him quicken himself to mercy and generosity. He that hath art and skill, let him do his best to share the use and utility thereof with his neighbor."